With eny b

John Mulray

THE TIME IS NOW

John Moloney

The Time is Now
THOUGHTS FOR THE DAY

the columba press

First published in 2001 by
the columba press
55A Spruce Avenue, Stillorgan Industrial Park,
Blackrock, Co Dublin

Cover by Bill Bolger
Origination by The Columba Press
Printed in Ireland by Colour Books Ltd, Dublin

ISBN 1 85607 333 5

Contents

Preface		9
1	A Blessing Of Hands	11
2	A Cross In The Forest	12
3	A Fresh Start	13
4	A Galilean Dawn	14
5	A Garden In Flower	15
6	A Heart For Now	16
7	A Hen And Her Chickens	17
8	A Hymn Of Praise	18
9	A Light In The Dark	19
10	A New Heart	20
11	A Pair Of Hands	21
12	A Patch Of Blue	22
13	A Rose Unpetalled	23
14	A Source Unending	24
15	A Watered Garden	25
16	All So Still	26
17	And He Went With Them	27
18	Angel Messengers	28
19	At Peter's Tomb	29
20	Before The Dawn	30
21	Before We Fall	31
22	Believing Is Seeing	32
23	Beneath The Deep	33
24	Bid Me Come To You	34
25	Book And Chalice	35
26	Boundless His Love	36
27	Bread Of The Word	37
28	City And Solitude	38
29	Collecting Our Needs	39
30	Come To Me	40
31	Entering His Presence	41
32	Eternal Memory	42
33	Evening To Remember	43

34	Examples Of Faith	44
35	Exploring The River	45
36	Facing The Rising Sun	46
37	Finding And Refinding	47
38	For Ever New	48
39	For Whom The Bell Tolls	49
40	Four Reasons For Loving	50
41	Freedom To Love	51
42	From Crib To Cross	52
43	Furnished And Ready	53
44	Gift From His Heart	54
45	Giving Thanks	55
46	God Exists	56
47	God's Masterpiece	57
48	He Sat Down	58
49	He Was Wounded	59
50	Heart For The Crowd	60
51	Immediately	61
52	In The Palm Of His Hand	62
53	Into Galilee	63
54	Just And Echo And A Fragrance	64
55	Just As I Am	65
56	Lest We Forget	66
57	Like A Rose Planted	67
58	Limping Across A Battlefield	68
59	Looking Towards Him	69
60	Love And Betrayal	70
61	Love That Conquers	71
62	Love Travels	72
63	Love Unloved	73
64	Mass At The Centre	74
65	Message In Marble	75
66	Moments Of Decision	76
67	Morning Has Broken	77
68	My Eyes And My Heart	78
69	O Saving Victim	79
70	On Every Road	80
71	Only Say The Word	81
72	Our Lady Of Knock	82
73	Over The Hills And Far Away	83
74	Perchance To Dream	84
75	Places To Remember	85

76	Power In Showing Mercy	86
77	Prayer Beyond Frontiers	87
78	Rejected By His Own	88
79	Remember Me	89
80	Rest A While	90
81	Revealed To Children	91
82	Sail On	92
83	Saint Joseph	93
84	Sight And Sound	94
85	Sign Of The Rainbow	95
86	Signposts For Eternity	96
87	Spreading The Good News	97
88	Stay Near Me	98
89	Sunset At Ballyconneely	99
90	The Good Shepherd	100
91	The Call	101
92	The Carpenter's Son	102
93	The Cherry Tree	103
94	The Contemplatives	104
95	The Cushion	105
96	The Diamond Rocks	106
97	The Divine Motherhood	107
98	The Drama Of Lovers	108
99	The Enigma Of Suffering	109
100	The Fifth Evangelist	110
101	The Final Triumph	111
102	The Four Freedoms	112
103	The Homecoming Of God	113
104	The Invisible Link	114
105	The Journey	115
106	The Landscape Painter	116
107	The Language Of Prayer	117
108	The Light Of Day	118
109	The Lights Of Home	119
110	The Lost Child	120
111	The Magnetism Of Love	121
112	The Missing Mail Bags	122
113	The Moment Of Parting	123
114	The Mystery Of The Missing Parcel	124
115	The Passion Play	125
116	The Peace Of Bethany	126
117	The Prayer Of Asking	127

118	The Prayer Of Childhood	128
119	The Prayer Of Twilight	129
120	The Question	130
121	The Rainboow Of Patience	131
122	The Reality Of Sin	132
123	The Refugee Road	133
124	The Reservoir	134
125	The Road Back	135
126	The Scruple	136
127	The Simple Things Of Life	137
128	The Stage Of Memory	138
129	The Storm	139
130	The Supper	140
131	The Testament	141
132	The Three Roads	142
133	The Trellis	143
134	The Wedding	144
135	The Winepress Alone	145
136	They Shall Look	146
137	Thirsting For Love	147
138	Tides	148
139	Tired From The Journey	149
140	To Give And To Belong	150
141	To Stay With Jesus	151
142	Today	152
143	Two Bridges	153
144	Two Messengers Of Mercy	154
145	Undimmed Memory	155
146	Up From The Dust	156
147	Wanting For Nothing	157
148	Watch For Boredom	158
149	Welcome Home	159
150	When Love Was Betrayed	160
151	Where The Beams Meet	161
152	Who Else Would Love?	162
153	Widen Your Hearts	163
154	Wings That Lift	164
155	With A Whole Heart	165

Preface

One tiny fragment of time is enclosed in the word 'Now'. A scripture phrase describes it: 'while today is still called today'. (Heb 3:13) Jesus announced his saving mission as belonging to today. 'Today this scripture has been fulfilled in your hearing.' (Lk 4:21)

The gospel tells us how Jesus used today. He was listening to pleadings for day to day needs – for food, for healing – and his response was always today. So often his day was a sequence of seemingly casual events: walking along the lakeside making his choice of disciples, a woman touching his garment, a spring flower evoking his admiration, the hospitality of Bethany friends, preparing breakfast for tired fishermen. He encountered them in the present tense, and through them he opened a vision of his heart.

Jesus is present, as in the gospel, in the now of our lives. These short reflections do not aspire to do more than humbly trying to interpret in his presence, a few of those events, insights, memories, which make up our day.

They are just random items: a conversation in a hospital ward, the view of sunset; a verse of a poem, the wisdom of a handicapped child, a missing parcel, a patch of blue sky, a visit to a Marian shrine, O Saving Victim, the drama of lovers, city and solitude, the carpenter's son, limping across a battlefield.

Each chapter stands by itself – just one theme, often led into by an illustration, one scripture quotation, closing with a line of a prayer.

They do not follow a pattern related to a liturgical time or feasts. They are simply a thought for the day when we might, in a quiet moment, withdrawn from outward things, open a page at random which could become a starting point for prayer, or an opening of a visit to the Blessed Sacrament.

We make time for the gaze of Jesus to rest on us, and our undivided attention to focus on him. He is master of time, and also servant of time, of our time.

At any moment of today he is available. We can isolate ourselves from the outside world and, without appointment, come into his presence. There, in an oasis of peace and quiet, we can enjoy with him an intimate, personal conversation.

The time is always now for us to spend even a few moments of each day with him, and thus develop an abiding awareness of his presence. So to make a reality the incredible dream 'to live through love in his presence'.(Eph 1:4)

John Moloney

A Blessing Of Hands

I had the privilege of officiating in a hospital at a ceremony of blessing of nurses' hands. In the presence of the Blessed Sacrament, over one hundred nurses came to the altar and opened their hands across which the Sign of the Cross was drawn; and then their hands were closed, as if reserved for a special purpose.

A nurse's hands speak a language of love. So many delicate gestures by her hands express a caring love for the sick – a hand placed on a forehead, a lift to a more comfortable position, a handclasp to reassure.

That language of love so tenderly expressed by nurses includes that whole world of caring love, exercised in so many settings – a mother's hands tending a handicapped child, the care of an ageing parent by one daughter of a family often sacrificing her freedom of choice of career. And then there is that great army of handmaids and brancardiers who tend the sick in the great Marian shrines.

They all must be inspired by the example which Jesus gave, how his hands expressed his love. 'He took her by the hand and the girl arose.' (Mt 9;23)

St Bernadette of Lourdes, as well as enduring sickness, also nursed the sick. Some one described her: 'She took my hands with all the tenderness of a mother.' An apt description of how the message of love is expressed by hands that nurse.

He stretched out his hand and touched him. (Mk 1:41)

Lord, make me generous in lending a hand to those in need.
Lord, bless all those whose hands reach out to care for the sick.

A Cross In The Forest

A young Indian girl, Kateri Tekakwitha, received the faith through the help of Jesuit missionaries in 1676. Her father was a Mohawk chief.

She would often accompany her family on riding expeditions through a forest, on towards Canada. On one such expedition she dismounted from her horse, and cut the Sign of the Cross on the bark of a tree. Then she knelt down in profound adoration of the crucified Jesus.

She developed a long and serious illness which she bore with remarkable courage and patience. She died at the age of twenty four.

Just a few years ago she was declared Blessed. At her beatification Pope John Paul II likened her as worthy to be considered among the great mystics, St Catherine of Siena, St Teresa of Avila and St Thérèse of the Child Jesus.

What a tribute! What a witness to the attraction of the cross! What an example for all of us, and perhaps of particular interest to youth.

Blessed Kateri teaches us a simple way of holiness – just to kneel, to look, to love, to adore Jesus crucified.

He loved me, and gave himself for me. (Gal 2:20)

I adore you, O Christ and praise you,
because by your holy cross you have redeemed the world.

A Fresh Start

Fishermen have keen knowledge of the sea, and how their prospects are affected by various factors – weather, light, seasons.

Simon and the apostles, after a fruitless night's fishing on the lake, had left their boats and were washing their nets. That was the moment when Jesus said to Simon, 'Launch out into the deep and let down your nets.' (Lk 5:4) From Simon came a two-fold response – the human reaction: 'Master, we toiled all night and took nothing.' (Lk 5:5). His experience of the lake, plus the previous night's failure, told him of little prospect of a catch. But then came the response of faith. 'But at your word, I will let down the nets.' (Lk 5:5) His obedience was typical of the childlike faith which would never desert him.

Again, there was an immediate response of Jesus to his faith. 'And when they had done this, they enclosed a great shoal of fish.' (Lk 5:6)

The two key phrases in this delightful story are the meeting place of the divine 'Launch out' and the human 'at your word'.

How often the defeat of work initiatives, the decline of apostolic projects, the falling apart of individual or family ventures, can bring a sense of disappointment. 'We have caught nothing.' That is the moment when we need the faith to hear again the words of Jesus, 'Launch out', and the courage, at his word, to let down the nets.

The next stage after a false start is a fresh start.

There is a saying of Fr Faber: 'We will discover, I believe, on the last day, that many heroic and saintly lives were simply a long chain of generous beginnings.'

Simon Peter … fell down at Jesus' knees, saying,
'Depart from me for I am a sinful man, O Lord.'
For he was astonished at the catch of fish. (Lk 5:8, 9)

Lord, give me courage when I fail; turn my weakness into strength so that I can make a fresh start. Bring to safety all who are storm-tossed.

A Galilean Dawn

In the calm of an Easter dawn on the lake of Galilee, men are pulling in to shore after a night's fishing. Coming near the land John was the first to recognise the risen Lord standing on the shore. With joy he cried out 'It is the Lord.' (Jn 21:7)

On a charcoal fire he had prepared a meal for them of bread and fish, and invited them, 'Come and have breakfast.' (Jn 21:12) And then, the exquisite final detail, he served it to them with his own hands. 'Jesus came and took the bread and gave it to them, and so with the fish.' (Jn 21:13) It is easy for us to discern the main features of the celebration of Sunday Mass against the background of that lakeside Easter scene.

Sunday means a pulling in to shore, a moment of rest that punctuates the rhythm of weekly work. At the centre is the risen Christ. Like the apostles, we recognise him with the eyes of faith, and proclaim, 'Christ has died; Christ is risen; Christ will come again.'

He has prepared divine food for us. He invites us to come and eat.

St Augustine calls Sunday 'A sacrament of Easter'. Sunday is the day of the Lord, his day in which he wishes to share with us the joy of his resurrection. It is important for us to keep him, as did the apostles, the Lord of the Day.

Just as day was breaking, Jesus stood on the beach. (Jn 21:4)

Lord Jesus, keep me faithful to my Sunday Mass, to be refreshed, and to receive the Bread of Life.
For all of us, may the Eucharist be the centre and summit of our Christian lives.

A Garden In Flower

At Pentecost the Holy Spirit came once for all. The wind of Pentecost is ever blowing through the Church, bringing a vivifying energy, a new fire of divine love. St Hippolytus describes the Church as 'the place where the Spirit flourishes'.

That flourishing makes present and visible the Church's faith, hope and charity, which are the supreme manifestations of the triumph of Jesus.

The Church's faith is clear and certain. It has no variations of rise or fall. Through it we become members of a great company of the 'faithful', capable of professing and living profound mysteries.

The Holy Spirit preserves for the Church the freshness of youth. It is like a garden in flower, in the variety and forms of religious life, and in the universal call to holiness.

Pope John Paul II describes the urgency of that call: 'Every lay Christian is an extraordinary work of God's grace, and is called to the heights of holiness.' To whatever age, whatever walk of life, the call goes out. In our response to that invitation there can be risings and fallings; sometimes, a sense of fatigue, a decline of conviction, a loss of the glow of love; just as in the universal Church, at this time, the pull of the world tending to prevail over the attraction of holiness.

There is always the need to reawaken the memory of Pentecost, to experience again the joy of the Spirit and the optimism of the Cross.

The Spirit of the Lord has filled the world. (Wis 1:7)

Come, Holy Spirit, fill the hearts of thy faithful.

A Heart For Now

'I am the Alpha and the Omega, the beginning and the end.' (Rev 5:6)
The love of Jesus for us spans our whole story from start to finish.
However we may fail to respond, one thing is certain. His love is for
all, and for always and for each, ever refreshing, healing, comforting. His heart is for now.

As he folds each of us in his embrace, so does he wish to embrace the whole human family.

Thus did Pope Leo XIII present the whole human family in a
solemn act of consecration to the Sacred Heart of Jesus in June,
1899. He was urged by 'a desire to provide a remedy for the evils
which afflict us, and which are increasing daily'. And, to provide
this remedy, he had recourse to the Heart of Jesus.

On the occasion of the centenary of that event, Pope John Paul
II wrote a letter presenting with the same sense of urgency the importance of devotion to the Sacred Heart of Jesus. He expressed his
'approval and encouragement to all who in any way continue to
foster, study, and promote devotion to the Heart of Christ'.

History repeats itself. The faith decline, dissent, confusion in
the last century are still around in our time. The same needs, the
same remedy. Christian family life needs support. Sacramental life
needs strengthening. The consecration of families to the Sacred
Heart nurtures the holiness of marriage, deepens the habit and
practice of prayer, makes the home a place where vocations to
priesthood and religious life can mature. Month by month the
Liturgy of the Heart of Jesus can help to restore and strengthen the
practice of frequent reception of the sacraments of Penance and the
Eucharist, and this, in turn, helps fidelity to Sunday Mass.

The time is now. His heart beats now, for he is ever near. For us
to make the commentary of our lives echo in response.

Abide in my love. (Jn 15:10)
Lord Jesus, give me a generous heart to respond each day to your love.

A Hen And Her Chickens

St Thérèse of the Child Jesus tells how, one day when she came upon a hen with her brood of chickens, she could not restrain her tears. That familiar sight reminded her of how intimate and complete is the love of Jesus for us, which enfolds us to himself. The words of Jesus came vividly to life for her at that moment.

'O Jerusalem, Jerusalem, killing the prophets and stoning those who are sent to you! How often would I have gathered your children together, as a hen gathers her brood under her wings, and you would not!' (Mt 23:37)

So many deep and consoling truths are presented by the familiar image of a hen and her brood of chickens.

The love of Jesus, so all-embracing. St Augustine says that there is no bird which conveys so completely the idea of an all-enfolding care. Her wings gather her whole brood till they are totally covered. Such is the spread of the love of Jesus for his whole flock.

The caring gesture of the hen is constantly repeated – an unending gathering. How often does Jesus extend his arms in a universal embrace; yet how often is his gesture rejected!

St John Chrysostom describes the pathos of that moment. 'Even the killing of the prophets could turn not my love away from you. And. not once but often, he shows the greatness of his love through the example of the hen.'

He was despised and rejected by men. (Is 53:3)

Lord Jesus, I pray you to enfold me each day in your protective embrace. Keep in your embrace all who are troubled.

A Hymn Of Praise

The highest expression of Beethovan's genius was his 'Choral Symphony', a majestic hymn of praise of creation.

Right through the psalms there are what are called 'the psalms of praise.' Psalm 148 very beautifully unfolds the way of praise. 'Praise the Lord, alleluia'.

The Lord deserves praise because of his mighty works, seen in his creation, and in his saving work. His overflowing love brought everything into existence. The whole of creation, a kind of spiritual stratosphere, is invited to praise the Lord – sun and moon and shining stars, waters above the heavens, fire and hail, snow and frost, mountains and hills and flying birds, young men and maidens, old men and women.

Then comes an unveiling: the Lord reveals his name: 'Let them praise the name of the Lord.'

And then comes the final unveiling. He reveals salvation.

To each of us comes the invitation constantly to make praise of the Lord part of our prayer.

I will praise you, Lord my God with all my heart,
and glorify your name for ever. (Ps 85:12)

Lord, help me to remember your saving love,
and to praise you every day.

A Light In The Dark

To travel along a narrow valley surrounded by mountains on a winter's night is an experience. Thick darkness coming down low, the mountain peaks like menacing shadowy figures ranged on either side. The sense of being alone on a lonely road. No sound except a whistling wind sweeping through the valley, no sign of life anywhere.

But then through the darkness comes a sign, a tiny light through the window of a little house set high up on the mountain. It brings a sense of companionship, the comfort of a presence that immediately restores the awareness of the consolation of light in the darkness.

In that house, perhaps an elderly person living alone, or a young family – no matter, that light tells that there, is life and heart and peace, not disturbed by a dark silent world outside in the valley.

That beam is a light shining in a dark place, a reminder of the light of faith that is always shining in a dark world. The light from the window of that little house is a symbol of the lives of those ordinary people who make no noise, and quietly live their faith, nourished by prayer and sacraments. They are not engaged in big affairs or projects, but they are an invaluable light in a world where a waning or uncertainty of faith brings darkening, insecurity, loneliness.

A little light through a window of a little house at Nazareth was enough to dispel the darkness, and restore the joy of companionship to a world in need of light.

He brought them out of darkness and gloom. (Ps 107:14)

Lord, be a light for my steps when darkness comes down.
Help all who are trying to discover the light of faith.
Give courage to those who are fearful of a journey by night.

A New Heart

A marvel of medical research and achievement in our time has been the success of heart transplant operations. Success depends on whether the patient accepts or rejects the new heart. Rejection means failure and the waning of hope of life.

In the world of the spiritual, the giving and receiving of a new heart is related to the highest expression of love.

In two directions the longing for a new heart is voiced. The Lord desires to give and receive love in abundance. His whole-hearted love deserves the response of receiving the whole heart. 'My son, give me your heart.' (Prov 23:26) Correspondingly he will give in abundance. 'I will give you a new heart.' (Ex 36:26)

There is the corresponding desire of the creature to respond with greater love. The great lovers keep pleading with the Lord, 'My heart is not capable of loving you as you deserve; would you give me your heart to love you with?'

I will give you a new heart, and a new spirit I will put within you.
(Ex 36:26)

Lord Jesus, make my heart like unto thine,
so that I may love you as you deserve.

A Pair Of Hands

A Canadian artist carved in wood a set of Stations of the Cross. He used only two beams of wood to present each station.

To present Simon of Cyrene carrying the cross behind Jesus, he showed a pair of hands holding the beam. But beneath the hands of Simon was another pair of hands, the hands of Jesus, upholding the hands of Simon.

How many services the hands of Jesus had performed – touching blind eyes, healing leprosy victims, raising a little girl to life, and taking her by the hand. And, then, the final service, at the supper, when he took bread in his hands, he blessed and broke it. One more gesture of love, when he was broken on the cross and his hands fastened, powerless, but yet powerful to lift a fallen world.

At some moment the burden of the cross may lie heavily on us. But however painful our journey, we know that the strong hands of Jesus are there to lift us.

A phrase of a hymn from the liturgy expresses our pleading to him in such a moment, 'Jesus, look towards me just as I am falling.'

Lifted by his hands we gain strength to follow his steps. The words of Fr James Brodrick SJ encourage us: 'A man's daily cross, composed of so many chips of frustration, boredom, weariness, pain, can crush him only if he forgets in whose footprints he is treading and whither going.'

The Lord's right hand has triumphed.
His right hand has raised me up. (Ps 117:16)

Lord Jesus, I beg you to ease the burden of my cross.
Give me your hand to clasp when I am falling.

A Patch Of Blue

A young Jewish girl, Anne Frank, had to take refuge with her family in an attic of an apartment in Amsterdam during World War II. She wrote a 'Diary' which tells the history of her family, restricted in one small living-room, in constant fear of being discovered, and ending in a concentration camp, which was her ultimate fate.

From her diary emerges a picture of a young girl, upright, courageous, grateful for small mercies. The attic of the apartment had one small window on the roof. Every day she thanked God for the view of just one patch of blue sky.

Surely, a story with a moral. Our life is a mozaic of small pieces – small events, casual encounters, the bonus of little gifts, a word, a help from a friend, a lift, a letter of support in time of trouble, the promise of a prayer – any of them can be part of just one day's experience.

A sensitivity for the small favours can make us wish not to let them go without a word of thanks. And it can draw us upwards to a continuous prayer of thanks for greater gifts he gives us every day.

I will give thanks to the Lord with all my heart. (Ps 110:1)

Give me, Lord, a grateful heart for all your favours.

A Rose Unpetalled

At the ceremony of the canonisation of St Thérèse of the Child Jesus, Pope Pius XI described her as 'an exquisite miniature of spiritual perfection', and proposed her *Little Way* of spiritual childhood as a way of holiness open to all of us. Two of her themes give us the key. Love means giving everything by giving one's self. It means to love Jesus and to make him loved.

Here is a verse of a poem, *A Rose Unpetalled,* which she composed shortly before her death, when she was suffering intense pain:

> Dear infant Christ, this fallen rose
> An image of that heart should be
> Which makes, as every instant flows,
> Its whole burnt-sacrifice to thee
> Upon thy altars, Lord, there gleams
> Full many a flower whose grand display
> Charms thee; but I have other dreams –
> Bloomless, to cast myself away.

She did not wish to be a rose in full bloom, but a 'rose unpetalled'. Like a faded petal she would cast herself away, just to be strewn on the path of the infant Jesus. She did not want the petals to be gathered to adorn an altar. Once she gave, she gave. She wanted nothing back.

Thérèse has taken the world by storm. Her *Little Way* looks easy, but not so easy to achieve. We need the power of her intercession.

A little child shall lead them. (Is 11:6)

St Thérèse of the Child Jesus, I ask your help to follow your Little Way on the road of love of Jesus.

A Source Unending

I know a valley in southern Italy, surrounded by mountains. High up on one mountain range there is a venerated shrine of Our Lady, Madonna of Canneto. And nearby, out of the ground, gushes up a spring of limpid clear water which is the source of a river that flows down into the valley, and is the only source of water to irrigate and sustain vegetation.

One is reminded of another source of life, from the heart of Jesus, an unending fountain of life.

It is useful for us to recall how two great lovers have used that image to describe the fountain of life and love that issues from his heart.

St Bonaventure: 'O water eternal and inaccessible, clear and sweet. Flowing from the spring that is hidden from the eyes of mortal men; whose depths cannot be plumbed … whose purity cannot be muddied. Because of this river which makes glad the city of God, we sing to you songs of thanksgiving and praise.'

St Margaret Mary reflects on the divine Heart from which issue three streams. The first is 'one of mercy for sinners, to which it brings in its flow the spirit of contrition and penance; the second stream is one of charity which flows to bring help to all those who are labouring under difficulties. The third stream flows with love and light to those who are God's perfect friends, whom he wishes to bring to complete union with himself.'

We need contantly to be refreshed at this unending source.

One of the soldiers pierced his side with a spear
and at once there came out blood and water. (Jn 19:34)

Heart of Jesus, pierced with a lance, have mercy on us.

A Watered Garden

In a garden, however small, we can experience peace and rest. In the silent presence of growth and beauty, we admire the harmony of colour, enjoy the fragrance, and we see the perfection of the divine workmanship, even in the tiny primrose in a crannied wall. We become conscious of how flowers respond to watering and to the sunlight.

St John of the Cross liked to picture the soul as like a garden, where the heavenly Father, like a gardener, takes delight in admiring the flowers, touching them here and there as he walks through the garden.

They are the virtues he finds in the soul, some in bloom, some fragile, some needing attention to survive.

His words are not just a figure of speech. They describe the reality. What virtues are in the soul were planted by the divine gardener, and only survive and grow by his daily care.

The prophet described the joy of the people whom God had ransomed, and used the figure of the garden to describe the divine intervention: 'They shall be radiant over the goodness of the Lord ... their life shall be like a watered garden.' (Jer 31:22, 13)

My beloved had a vineyard ... and planted it with choice vines.
(Is 5:1, 2)

Lord, I thank you for your daily care of me.

All So Still

He came all so still
Where his mother was
As dew in April
That falleth on the grass.

No sound of trumpet to announce his coming. No clarion call to proclaim his message. Through a mother, pondering the word, he came in the silence of the night.

When night was on its way, and all things were in silence the divine Word-made-flesh came into this world. All so still, noiseless as the dew falling on the grass.

And, surrounded by that blessed stillness, his life unfolded. Just once only his voice was heard, when in the temple he explained his absence. From then there was the stillness of Nazareth. We can imagine those lovely Nazareth evenings with Mary and Joseph, as they would point out Mount Carmel to him, and explain how, there, Elijah had heard the voice of God, 'in the rustle of a gentle breeze.' (1 Kgs 19:12)

In his public life, while he was in the midst of crowds, he safeguarded his solitude.

St Ignatius of Antioch emphasises the importance of the contemplative dimension of the life of Jesus. 'Anyone who truly possesses the words of Jesus will also be able to hear his silence ... that he may act through his words and be known through his silence.'

Our world is afraid of silence. It tries to find companionship through noise. We have to follow and find Jesus in his avenues of silence. Fr Sertillanges OP reminds us that 'even in the excitement of his active life, there were hidden depths full of silence where his interior life expanded at a profound level, and whose external action was but a delicate veil.'

When evening came he was there alone. (Mt 14:23)

Lord Jesus, help us to create a zone of silence round our hearts, and there to find you.

And He Went With Them

A short phrase of Pope John Paul II, 'Love travels', says much in a few words. It enters into some lovely gospel events. They might be called a sequence: crisis, appeal, response.

Love responds to need. It doesn't wait till tomorrow.

For Jairus came a crisis. His daughter is in danger of death. He makes an urgent appeal to Jesus, 'Come'. And then came the immediate response. 'And he went with them.' (Mk 5:24) How impressive was the response of Jesus! He followed after. He became obedient to need.

There is a parallel moment – a centurion's servant on the point of death. Again, the crisis is presented, followed by an urgent appeal 'they besought him urgently.' (Lk 7:4) And again, the same calm, immediate answer to need: 'Jesus went with them.' (Lk 7:6)

A third time it is different. This time the crisis is a world in need of salvation. Jesus, responding to that need 'went out bearing his own cross.' (Jn 19:17) Love travelled. Well for us!

The gospel belongs to now. As along the roads of Galilee, life is punctuated with urgent calls. And love still travels. It touches down on the roadside of down-and-outs.

Love prompts us to follow the example of Jesus who 'went with' people in trouble. And even if the problem is too deep for us to give more than limited help, our compassion and presence can bring relief.

He heals the brokenhearted. (Ps 147:3)

Lord Jesus, open my heart to the needs of those in trouble.
Bring them the consolation of your healing love.

Angel Messengers

The *Catechism of the Catholic Church* explains the mission of angels. 'From the Incarnation to the Ascension, the life of the Word incarnate is surrounded by the adoration and service of angels.'

In his coming into the world and at his departure, they offered him adoration. And we find them engaged in service, in the central events in which they have been 'messengers of his saving plan'.

The angel Gabriel was sent from God to announce the mystery of the Incarnation. He was the first to look in wonderment on the beauty of Mary, and to hear her word of acceptance of the divine motherhood.

As Mary was alone, Jesus was alone in the garden when an angel came to strengthen him in that dread hour.

On Easter morning the first news of his resurrection was given by two angels dressed in white. They gave Mary Magdalene and the women a message to convey to Peter and the apostles: 'Go, tell his disciples and Peter that he is going before you to Galilee.' (Mk 12:7) Angels were the first messengers of the resurrection of Jesus.

And again, at the moment of his Ascension, are two angels dressed in white robes. And to them also is given the honour of handing on the final message before the Lord's departure: 'This Jesus, who was taken up from you into heaven, will come in the same way as you saw him go.' (Acts 1:11)

In the revelation of joy, sorrow, glory, in the drama of salvation, the service of angels has been important. So also must be the power of their intercession. We can profit by invoking their help when we come to the celebration of the holy Eucharist.

Praise him, all his angels. (Ps 148:2)

Lord, send your holy angels to help me to adore and serve.
May the joyful message of angels gladden all hearts.

At Peter's Tomb

Down through the centuries countless people have knelt at the tomb of St Peter to profess their faith and ask for a refreshment of faith.

At the beginning of the Millennium year, Pope John Paul II spoke of the masterpiece in the Sistine Chapel that presents the conferral of the keys on St Peter. 'In this painting the artist, through the symbol of the enormous key, stresses the breath of authority conferred on Peter. On the other hand Peter's face is depicted with a moving expression of humility as he receives the symbol of his ministry, on his knees and almost drawing back from his Master. His wrapt expression prompts us to imagine on his lips not only the confession of Caesarea Philippi, 'You are 'the Christ, the Son of the living God' (Mt 16:16), but also the declaration of love he made to the risen Christ after the sorrowful experience of his denial: 'You know that I love you.' (Jn 21:15)

We may not have the opportunity of kneeling at Peter's tomb, but we can place ourselves in his company, often asking him to pray for us that we might, with deep conviction, repeat his confession of faith, and his profession of love.

You are Peter, and on this rock I will build my Church. (Mt 16:18).

Lord, through the intercession of St Peter, strengthen my faith and love.

Before The Dawn

'The darkest hour is that before the dawn.'

A night of pain and restlessness without sleep, the ache of a persistent problem, seem harder to bear through that late hour before the dawn comes. Somehow, with the first sign of morning light, there can come some sense of relief.

The darkest hour, described by the poet, seems to fit the experience of the apostles on the lake of Galilee by night. The story is told in detail. It was the darkest hour – 'the fourth watch', that is, about five in the morning. The boat was beaten by waves. (Mt 14:24) 'They were distressed in rowing, for the wind was against them.' (Mk 6:48)

At that dark moment Jesus came 'walking on the sea'. At first, not recognising him, they were terrified. 'But immediately he spoke to them saying, "Take heart, it is I; have no fear".' (Mt 14:27). St John Chrysostom says, 'Immediately they recognised his voice, they were healed.'

Are they not a graphic description of our efforts to cope with pain or problem, through what seems an never-ending night? We are 'distressed'. We can make no headway.

Like the apostles we cry out for help to the Lord. How often when we felt overcome, Jesus has come to our rescue, walking on the waters, and given us the same reassuring message, 'Take heart, it is I; have no fear.'

And he got into the boat with them and the wind ceased. (Mk 6:51)

Lord Jesus, I pray you to come to me
in a dark night when I am distressed, and take away my fears.

Before We Fall

Here is a little drama in a kitchen. A small child climbs his way to the top of a table, while his mother is occupied nearby. He loses his balance and is falling to the ground. But in that split second his mother puts her hand beneath his head before he hits the ground.

It is an example of that instant and instinctive intervention of a mother to protect her child from harm. She does not need to have training; it is built in her possession of mother love.

That little drama brings to mind Mary's immediate response to need. 'Rising up, she went with haste.' (Lk 1:39) Her mother love answers a need then and always.

Two descriptions, in words of surpassing beauty, tell of her interventions.

The Advent hymn, *Alma Redemptoris,* addresses her. 'O loving Mother of the Redeemer ... help your people in their risings and their fallings.' How many fallings her people risk; how many fallings are we all prone to, when we need her strong arms to lift us lest we crash.

In the closing canto of the *Paradiso,* Dante addresses Mary: 'Your loving kindness helps us, not only when we call, but often you freely answer our requests before we ask.'

She anticipates our need. Her watchful care of us is so alert that she is beside us even before our need arises.

Mary...wrapped him in swaddling clothes,
and laid him in a manger. (Lk 1:7)

O loving Mother, bring relief and lift all
who fall beneath various burdens and disasters,
and obtain for all of us the grace to avoid falling into sin.

Believing Is Seeing

A group of young children approached the grotto at Lourdes hold-ing each other's hands. A sister led them to the grotto. They stood motionless before the statue of Our Lady. They were all blind.

Just then a group of German pilgrims was singing the verse of the hymn *Ave maris stella:* 'Ave, Star of ocean ... give sight to the blind ... show yourself our Mother ... till we gaze on Jesus, and re-joice for ever.'

Mary had been declared by Elizabeth: 'Blessed is she who be-lieved.' (Lk 1:45)

How often would she hear her son praise the faith of those whom he would heal. How readily he responded to a prayer of faith. When a woman pleaded with him to cure her daughter, he said, 'O woman, great is your faith! Be it done for you as you de-sire.' (Mt 14:28)

All of us, both child and adult, have need of and are enriched by the prayer of faith.

This is the victory that overcomes the world, our faith. (1 Jn 5:4)

Lord, I believe; help my unbelief.

Beneath The Deep

There has been an urge to try to locate ships which through accident or war sank beneath the deep. Many such efforts have been successful.

The *Titanic,* on its maiden voyage, through an accidental impact with an iceberg, was found resting on the seabed. A US warship, sunk in the naval battle of Mid Way, has been located.

Men who had been on opposite sides in war, stood in friendship together over where the ship had been sunk. There was about that occasion a sense of achievement, a recall of memories, as well as an experience of sadness for the loss of comrades.

There is another exploration with a different purpose and achievement. It is what St Paul calls searching the unfathomable depths of the love of Jesus. And because the love of his heart is without limits, there is no end to 'the depth of the riches and wisdom and knowledge of God', (Rom 11:33) still to be sounded.

We can read the words of St John of the Cross in this context. 'There are depths to be fathomed in Christ. He is like a rich mine with many recesses containing treasures, and no matter how men try to fathom them the end is never reached. Rather, in each recess, men keep on finding here and there new veins of new riches.'

Each of us is not only able but invited to travel the inward journey of adventure to the heart of Jesus; and having been enriched by the experience of his love, we are drawn to return. For here is a source of unending refreshment.

That you ... may have the power to comprehend with all the saints what is the breadth and length and height and depth, and to know the love of Christ ... (Eph 3:17-19)

Lord Jesus, open my heart to respond to the unfathomable riches of your love.

Bid Me Come To You

Pope Paul VI presented a theme for reflection for a Eucharistic Congress in South America, 'Bid me come to you.'

The setting in which those words were spoken was the lake of Galilee on a night when Peter and the apostles were out on a boat.

Jesus came, walking on the waters. At first they were terrified, not recognising him. But immediately he said to them to take heart, Peter answered him, 'Lord, if it is you, bid me come to you on the water.' So Peter got out of the boat and walked on the water and came to Jesus; but when he saw the wind, he was afraid, and beginning to sink, he said, 'Lord, save me.' (Mt 14:28-31)

The human heart has the urge to come close to the Lord who comes, and remains in his eucharistic presence. But to reach him we need to cross that dark ocean where the tide of the world, with fears and failures and confusions, can be running against us.

We will not be engulfed once we lift our eyes above them, and fix them on Jesus. To all of us there is an ever-repeated invitation to come into his eucharistic presence. Recognising and finding him, we will find the same spontaneous expression of faith with which the apostles greeted him when he entered the boat: 'Truly, you are the Son of God.' (Mt 14:33)

Jesus immediately reached out and caught him, saying to him,
'O man of little faith, why did you doubt?' (Mt 14:31)

Lord Jesus, I thank you for your presence in the Eucharist,
and for reaching out to us when the trials of life assail us.

Book And Chalice

Speaking to pilgrims, Pope John XXIII told of his first visit to the Basilica of St John Lateran after he became Pope. He was greeted by the Archpriest of the Basilica, who gave him two gifts, 'The Book' and 'The Chalice', saying to him, 'These are the two things which every person needs.'

Both represent, in the celebration of the Eucharist, what are called 'the Table of the Word' and 'the Table of the Bread', which combine to form one act of worship.

In the Word, God speaks to us as friends, and his word is always new, fresh, and related to the now of our lives. Our response is meant to be an active listening, what Romano Guardini calls, 'the stillness before God, the quiet at the depths of life's inner stream, a being "all there", receptive, alert.'

In the Liturgy of the Eucharist, the sacrifice of Calvary is sacramentally renewed; Jesus offers himself up together with the Church. His Body 'given up', and then, given back. 'Take, all of you and eat.'

Thus, through the Book and the Chalice, we are enriched. We can hope to become what we receive.

He who eats this bread will live for ever. (Jn 6:58)

Lord Jesus, I pray you to open my mind to your word, and my heart to receive you worthily in the Eucharist.

Boundless His Love

We have been fascinated by the exploration and conquest of space in our time. We have been made aware of that vast world of planets now being reached.

There is another conquest in the realm of faith that fills us with wonder. St Bernard describes it: 'Boundless in time and space he loves us. Shall we set boundaries to his love?' His words express a challenge and open up to us a vision of God who reveals a love without limits.

In the life of Jesus on earth even a couple of examples express his boundless love. There was no road he would not travel to hand on his message. 'To other cities' he must go. No malady that his healing hand would not reach. 'He went about ... healing every manner of disease and every infirmity among the people.' (Mt 3:23) His final proof of limitless love came when he extended his arms on the cross, from east to west, to heal the whole human family.

The love that touched St Bernard and made his life a love-song, evoked a like response from the heart of a young girl from the same region of France eight hundred years later. Elizabeth of the Trinity was entranced by the thought of the limitless love of Jesus. 'How rich God is in mercy. With what an excess of love he loves us!' (Eph 2:4) St. Paul's phrase 'excess of love' became the theme that directed her life. She said, 'There is a word of Paul that is like a summary of my existence, that could be written over each moment of my life: "because of his excessive love.".Yes, all the graces of my life – they arise from his having loved me all too much.'

For Bernard, love, boundless; for Elizabeth, excessive. Shall we set limits?

> **But God, who is rich in mercy, out of the excessive love**
> **with which he has loved us ... (Eph 2:4)**

> *Lord Jesus, make my heart ever more generous*
> *in responding to your boundless love of me.*

Bread Of The Word

It has been said that 'education is truth in a state of transmission'. There is a movement from the teacher who transmits to the hearer who learns.

Jesus came to do and teach.

One day a great throng gathered round him. He had compassion on them because they were hungry, and he gave them food. His heart also went out to them because 'they were like sheep without a shepherd, and began to teach them many things.' (Mk 6:34) He fed them with the bread of the word.

Only a few days before his death 'every day he was teaching in the temple'. (Lk 21:37) Even though he knew that the plot to destroy him was completed, he never ceased handing on the truth. And we are told that, 'all the people came to him in the temple to hear him'. (Lk 22:38)

So, the Church remains faithful to its teaching mission. It keeps 'teaching daily', and its message is for 'all the people', day after day, century after century, always fresh and new, a lamp for our steps, presenting the splendour of the truth.

And, as in the temple, we, a redeemed people, through the power of the Holy Spirit, are able to 'hear' the truth; we can grasp the most profound mysteries, and accept them with joy.

We can rejoice in the gospel message because it is 'The Good News'.

Go ... teaching them to observe all that I have commanded you.
(Mt 28:20)

Lord, help us to be always attentive and faithful to your teaching.

City And Solitude

It is said that everyone has need of city and solitude. That means the need of companionship within a community, and, as well, the possibility of withdrawing alone into a haven of quiet, not pursued by the noises of the world.

It is useful for us to place the idea of city and solitude in the setting of our Christian life.

The city is the assembly, gathered for the celebration of the Eucharist. Here we become part of a great company, members of the worshipping family, gathered round the altar. Voices become one in expressing prayer of praising and pleading. That union is completed through sacramental communion, when we share the life-giving Bread, and become vitally united with one another.

Solitude. We also have need of that quiet space where we meet the Lord in the intimacy of a personal conversation, as friend talking to friend.

The *Catechism of the Catholic Church* presents the idea of a 'prayer corner' with the sacred scriptures and icons, in order to be there, in secret, before our Father. In a Christian family, this kind of little oratory fosters prayer in common.

City and solitude are closely linked. Each supports and enriches the other.

When you pray, go into your room and shut the door
and pray to your Father who is in secret. (Mt 6:6)

Lord, help me to find you in personal prayer,
and so enrich my participation in the celebration of the Eucharist.

Collecting Our Needs

In the world of business a project can follow a pattern – preparation, procedure, prospect of attaining goals.

The Prayers (Collects) of the Sunday Masses are very rich in content. They gather or collect the varied strands of our needs, and present them in concise form to the Lord. An example is the Prayer of the 20th Sunday of the year. We might reflect on it under three headings: promise, preparation, prize.

Promise: 'Lord God, you have promised for those who love you, what no eye has seen nor ear heard.' The promise carries just one condition – 'for those who love you' – to a reward beyond all human expectations.

Preparation: 'Fill our hearts with your love, so that loving you above all and in all ...' We are not capable of making a worthy response of love. We need you to fill our hearts with a love that is whole-hearted.

Prize: 'We may attain your promises which the heart of man has not conceived.' Then we can dare to win fulfilment of your promise – the prize beyond all our dreams.

I will sing for ever of your love, O Lord. (Ps 88:1)

Lord, help me to love you with all my heart,
and so become worthy of your promised reward.

Come To Me

What a lovely word is 'Come'! It tells of an open heart, an open door. It easily leads to 'Welcome'.

It is almost like the gilded cover of the opening and closing chapters of the drama of salvation: the start: 'Come and see' (Jn 1:39), the close: 'Come, Lord Jesus.' (Rev 22:20) And in the early moments of the public life of Jesus, we find it again: 'Come to me.'

That moment described by St Matthew is regarded as the first explicit revelation of the love of the heart of Jesus. He turned to thank his Father for revealing to babes what is concealed from the wise. Such is the gracious will of his Father.

And then, the invitation, 'Come to me, all who labour and are heavy laden, and I will give you rest.' (Mt 11:28) 'To me', your destination is my heart. 'All who labour' – the vast, restless throng of humanity, each without exception. St John Chrysostom explains: 'He did not say "you and you", but "all" you who are lonely, sad, or in sin; not just to relieve the strain, but that I might forgive your sins.'

'Learn of me, for I am gentle and lowly of heart, and you will find rest for your souls.' (Mt 11:29) He who has taken the whole burden of sin on his shoulders, and is ever easing that dead weight of human suffering, and yet remains gentle and patient, is our teacher. He eases the burdens which others place on us, and those we place on others.

The invitation of Jesus to come to him crosses all frontiers of time and space. It echoes down those dark valleys of our lives when our burden seems to have no therapy, and we find we can go no further. 'Come to me.' Just to remember that invitation and that message. What relief! What support!

Come to me ... and you will find rest for your souls. (Mt 11:29)

Heart of Jesus, of whose fullness we have all received,
have mercy on us.

Entering His Presence

To dress for an occasion is more than a convention. It is an expression of regard for the occasion, and for the person who invites us.

To answer the invitation of Jesus to come into his eucharistic presence deserves special preparation.

Two experts in love can help us.

St Jerome: 'He teaches us and makes us a garment white as snow; and when he clothes us in his own garment, then he gives us nourishment.' The sacrament of Penance effects a constant cleansing of our souls, and makes us all the more worthy to come into his presence, and to be nourished.

Putting aside alien affections and cleansing themselves, then the people would be ready for a change of garments.

St John of the Cross: He recalls the moment when Jacob desired to ascend Mount Bethel to build an altar for the offering of sacrifice to God. He first ordered the people to do three things: to destroy all strange gods, to purify themselves, and to change their garments. (Gen 35:2) Then their souls will be clothed in God, in a new understanding of God, and in a new love of God.

Just as the people were worthy to climb Mount Bethel, so we become worthy to come to the altar to worship and adore the Lord.

He has clothed me with the garments of salvation. (Is 61:10)

Lord, make me worthy to come into your presence.

Eternal Memory

Some people have an exceptional gift of very retentive memory. They can recall past events in detail. Across the span of years they can remember your name.

How can we not marvel at the divine memory? The following psalm is an entrance antiphon for the Mass of the Sacred Heart of Jesus: 'The thoughts of his heart last through every generation, that he will rescue them from death and feed them in time of famine.' (Ps 32:11, 19)

His thoughts last, his memory is everlasting, stronger and more tender than a mother remembering her child. With the passage of time from one generation to another, his memory and his love never fade.

His thoughts, springing from his heart, are not static; they are active in our regard. They are the source of life. 'From his wounded side flowed blood and water, the fountain of sacramental life in his church.'

Two sacraments nearest to our day-to-day needs:

'...to deliver them from death' – life refreshed or restored, in the sacrament of Penance.

'... to feed them in time of famine', through the Eucharist. He remembers his giving; we remember his gifts with thanks.

Remember your mercy, Lord,
and the love you have shown from of old. (Ps 25:6)

Lord Jesus, help me to grow in your love
through the sacraments of Penance and the Eucharist.
Through this Fountain of Life may all hearts be refreshed!

Evening To Remember

It is said that one gospel phrase can change a whole life. So it did for Andrew and his companion when the shadow of Jesus crossed their path for the first time. We would do well to dwell on the details of this fascinating story line by line.

John the Baptist pointed to Jesus as he passed, 'and they followed Jesus'. (Jn 1:37) Already, before they saw him, there were the stirrings of an attraction to him, the beginnings of a vocation.

'Jesus turned.' (Jn 1:38) When Jesus turns, there is always a special meeting, a specific message. He saw them. When he looks, he looks into the heart; one look could warm to love, or melt to tears.

Then two questions. 'What do you seek? Where are you staying?' And then the invitation, 'Come and see.' (Jn 1:38, 39)

The Fathers of the Church interpret those words – 'Come' as the activity, and 'See' as the contemplation. 'Come' is the marketplace, and 'See' is the desert. Come, and as reward for your coming, then you will see.

'They stayed with him that day.' (Jn 1:39) St Augustine invites us: 'Let us build a dwelling in our hearts where he may come and teach us.'

We cannot pierce the veil that hides the marvel of that evening. We would like, in the phrase of St John of the Cross, 'to tear through the veil of that sweet encounter to find the living flame of love that tenderly wounded.'

When we come to stay with Jesus in his eucharistic presence, might we ask him to make audible his invitation, 'Come and see', to young hearts in the freshness of springtime, to hearts famished with a deep hunger for God, to hearts struggling in a torment of doubt, trying to resolve the seeming enigma of existence.

And they stayed with him that day, for it was about the tenth hour.
(Jn 1:39)

Lord, bid me stay with you always.

Examples Of Faith

To gain acceptance of an idea or a project, to convey its importance, various approaches are often used. There can be continued repetition, presenting it from various angles and different settings, showing how its acceptance can bring success and reward.

The author of the Letter to the Hebrews presents the importance of the virtue of faith, necessary for assurance and conviction. In chapter eleven he lists eleven outstanding examples of faith, right across the history of salvation.

There was the acceptable sacrifice of Abel, Enoch rewarded for pleasing God by his faith, Noah took heed of God's plan to rescue his people, the total obedience of Abraham, Sarah received power to conceive, Isaac invoked blessings on Jacob, Jacob blessed the sons of Joseph, Moses left Egypt and kept the Passover, Rahab gave hospitality. Then there were Gideon, David, Samuel, as well as very many men and women who suffered, mocking, scourging, torture.

Such a variety of witnesses with one quality which united them, their intrepid faith!

Let us run with perseverance,
looking to Jesus the pioneer and perfecter of our faith. (Heb 12:2)

Lord, increase my faith.
Enrich all people with the gift of faith.

Exploring The River

To explore a river is to make a journey of adventure. One can trace its movement through plains and woodlands and towns, to notice how it is a source of life for the terrain through which it passes. One intriguing thing about a river is that it never dries up

There are two ways to follow it: either from its source, perhaps a little spring or rivulet coming down from the hills as it wends its way outwards to the sea, or one can start back from its mouth along to its source.

There is a river, the great River of Life, that starts from the Heart of Jesus. 'From his wounded side there flowed out blood and water, a fountain of sacramental life in the Church.' From there comes the sevenfold gift of sacraments, spaced along our pilgrim journey that meets our every moment and need.

We can likewise reflect on the movement of his heart, travelling back to the source of life-giving graces, for restoring, comforting ,encouraging, that enrich us beyond measure.

We become more keenly aware of his boundless love, like a great river in flood, which is infinitely available.

St Gregory of Nyssa reminds us that 'you may trace a river to its source, but you cannot exhaust its source'.

To come to the Heart of Jesus is to begin to try to fathom, at source, the unfathomable depths of his love. Our response is limited, but it can open out in a love ever more generous, for his heart is ever open to us.

Out of his heart shall flow rivers of living water. (Jn 7:37)

Lord, refresh me at the fountain of your heart.

Facing The Rising Sun

To stand in the early morning facing the Roman Basilica of St John Lateran is a memorable experience. The sun coming up from behind the Alban hills plays on the massive façade. Facing the rising sun, clear cut against a cloudless sky, stand enormous statues representing Our Lord with the Cross beside him, and the apostles ranged in a line on either side with him. The whole scene speaks of victory and of life and of an eternal pasch.

It recalls the glory of the risen Lord, but it also tells the story of the passion of his infant Church, and her first great resurrection in him. After an incredible endurance of successive persecutions, the Christian community emerged from the catacombs, and the building of a church of St John Lateran signalled the beginning of a new world.

The Church came out into the light of day, and this basilica rose up, stone upon stone, as the scattered remains of the temples of the pagan gods were strewn around the Roman Forum.

But it is on the living stones of living faith that the Church has been built up. The same faith brings together a mighty concourse of pilgrims every year for the eucharistic celebration of the feast of Corpus Christi in the Basilica of St John Lateran.

Like living stones be yourselves built into a spiritual house.
(1 Peter 2:5)

Lord, strengthen my faith in and love for the Church.

Finding And Refinding

We can use the word 'find' in a general sense, for instance, finding a lost object, or meeting a person by accident. Or, we may set out with the purpose of meeting a person whom we have decided to find.

The gospel tells of a finding, 'The next day Jesus decided to go to Galilee, and he found Philip and said to him, "Follow me".' (Jn 1:43) That finding had a special meaning. It was not as if Jesus happened to be passing that way, and by accident met Philip.

Jesus, of set purpose, 'found' Philip. He had found him from all eternity. This finding set up a new relationship. A new world for Philip, a vocation to apostleship. Immediately he was on the road to convey the good news to Nathaniel. Later he would be approached by the Greeks with a request: 'We wish to see Jesus.' (Jn 12:21) The apostle who had been found was given the request to find Jesus. He went and told Andrew, who had been the first apostle to have found the Messiah, and both of them went to Jesus. 'Andrew went with Philip and they told Jesus.' (Jn 1:22) The story contains the sequence of finding and refinding.

It tells our own history. Each of us has been 'found' by Jesus, and our life has been a repeated refinding of him. We can make our own the words of Pascal: 'You would not go on seeking him if you had not already found him.' Finding him has meant a deepening of our knowledge and love of him, which carries us ever onward on that great adventure. There is the unending joy, expressed by the spouse in the Canticle, 'I have found him whom my soul loves.' (Song 3:4) Our prayer shall be that he would 'find' us at the end.

Philip found Nathaniel. (Jn 1:45)

*Lord Jesus, I know that you would not have sought me
if you had not found me. Help me to find you with joy each day,
and love you ever more and more.*

For Ever New

What is new attracts. Those who are in the world of marketing make the most of exploiting that attraction. A brand new model for you! You must have it!

Jesus brought all newness into the world by bringing himself. While he is like us in all things except sin, there is a quality of his which might be called his uniqueness, his specialness, his eternal newness.

A monk of the Eastern Church has aptly described this trait: 'Jesus communicated to everything round him something of his own personal newness. A kind of new integrity, characterises many things which touch his life and with which he comes in contact.'

A gospel incident illustrates this. While he was at supper, a woman entered and brought a vase of precious ointment, poured the whole contents on his head, and then broke the vase. It had fulfilled a sacred purpose, and must not revert back to common usage.

He would ride into Jerusalen on a colt on which no one had ever sat. (Lk 19:30) On his way to Calvary the tunic he wore was without seam. (Jn 19:21) And he who brought newness of life, by his death was laid in a tomb where no one had ever been laid. (Jn 19:41)

So also should our love be if it is to be worthy of him. It should have the quality of newness, something apart, reserved for him alone.

O sing to the Lord a new song. (Ps 95:1)

Lord, keep my love for you special with the freshness of a new song.

For Whom The Bell Tolls

There is an impressive story from Yugoslavia, where faith and freedom had been severely repressed for many years. When their church was forcibly closed, during those dark years, the people of a certain village buried their church bell in the ground.

After freedom was restored they dug up the bell and hung it on the branch of a tree and rang it. The peal of that bell was both a symbol and an invitation and call to celebrate the Eucharist again in freedom.

Often in the casting of bells two words were inscribed: *'Vox Dei'*, 'the voice of God'.

The Sunday Mass bell tolls through our land. Sounding through highways and byways, through the streets of cities and villages, across the hills and valleys of the countryside. It is like the invitation in the gospel parable to go out on to the highways and byways to announce that the banquet is ready.

It invites us to makes space, to slow down the busy rhythm of work, to turn down the volume, so that our ears can be alert and respond to the voice of God who speaks to us in the act of worship. Our Sunday Mass bell invites us to create around us a zone of silence.

There was a time in our land when the bell was forced to remain silent, yet the call to celebrate the Eucharist echoed in faithful hearts.Now it can sound again and it says 'Come' – everyone, youth and adult, a personal invitation to all. It is a call to universal Christian families in every land.

He sat at table, and the disciples with him. (Lk 22:14)

Lord, give us this bread always.

Four Reasons For Loving

Very simply the psalmist lists four reasons why we should break out into a song of love. He enters into the realities of our daily life with its varied problems, and then invites us to express our thanks, and gives us a formula to put our love into words.

In descriptive terms he describes the love which the Lord displays in meeting all our needs. (Ps 17:1-3)

My strength: the burdens of life weigh down on me and sap my strength. But you turn my weakness into strength. I love you, Lord.

My rock: You give me a rock to rest on, you place a rock beneath my feet, so that my feet don't slip as I walk on solid ground. I love you, Lord.

My fortress: You shelter me, like an army that finds refuge when under attack. I love you, Lord.

My saviour: You save me because you love me.

How can I not express my love of my Lord, who in every moment of danger comes to my rescue?

'The Lord is worthy of all praise.' Coming to meet all my needs, the Lord deserves the fullness of praise from a grateful heart.

From his temple he heard my voice. (Ps 17:6)

Lord, I thank you for all your saving help.
Protect all who are in danger or in trouble.

Freedom To Love

O God I love you
Because you have first loved me.
I deprive myself of freedom,
So that, chained to you,
I may follow you.

This verse of a Latin hymn is rich in meaning. How well it summarises the whole mystery of life and love!

God whose very name is love, having given himself to me, has no more to give.

Not only has he loved me first, before I thought of responding, but he loves me always.

Faith makes me capable of tracing the gift of your love to its source. The drama, Lord, begins with you.

You have first loved me, long before I thought of loving you. Before I had a memory, your love has been with me, not for a day or a year but an everlasting gift.

The sheer marvel of your limitless love challenges me to open my heart in a response, however feeble. As a start I thank you for your boundless love of me, and ask you to deepen my understanding that the science of love is in giving rather than in having.

I deprive myself of freedom. I start by trying to free myself from the things which the world tells me I need. I try to make myself free from false freedom so that I can hand myself over to you. Then I can be free to follow you, chained to you, not by chains that imprison, but by chains of love.

I led them with cords of compassion,
with bands of love. (Hos 11:4)

Lord, draw me to love you more and more.

From Crib To Cross

In the Eastern Church there is a practice at Christmas of embroidering on the swaddling clothes the Sign of the Cross. Also, the figure of the Divine Infant is presented with arms extended as he would be on the Cross.

In those symbolic ways is presented the unity of the mystery of redemption. From the wood of the crib to the wood of the cross, the mystery is one. The poverty, the abandonment, the rejection which Jesus suffered on the Cross, he already experienced at his coming.

No royal home but a cross. The closed doors already prefigure the abandonment of Calvary. So quickly after his coming came the shedding of the blood of innocent children. Later he, the innocent Lamb, would shed his own blood.

Just as beneath the Cross there was the comfort of loving hearts, so at Bethlehem he was greeted with the joyful welcome of pure hearts and the song of angels.

Not long after his coming he was on the road to exile, who at Calvary would welcome all of us, exiles, home.

When we celebrate his coming every year with special solemnity, we greet him with the age old song, *'Venite adoremus'*, 'Come, let us adore him.'

Beneath the Cross, our prayer of worship is the same: 'We adore thee, O Christ and praise thee.'

In our lives, punctuated by the interplay of Bethlehem joy and Calvary sorrow, we are certain that the same love that made him come and made him die for us, is always beside us.

His name shall be called Emmanuel, (which means, God with us).
(Mt 1:23)

Lord, on the road of life each day, stay close by me.
Ease the cross of those who are burdened with illness, stress, loneliness.

Furnished and Ready

Before a project in the world of business is undertaken there is generally careful preparation.

The divine preparation for central events in the history of salvation had a particular pattern. It was never hurried; there was careful attention to detail; it had the quality of reverence for the events that lay ahead.

When the supreme moment of his life was approaching, Jesus prepared. 'So Jesus sent Peter and John, saying, "Go and prepare the passover for us that we may eat it." They said to him, "Where will you have us prepare it?" He said to them, 'Behold when you have entered the city a man carrying a jar of water will meet you; follow him into the house where he enters, and tell the householder, 'The Teacher says to you, where is the guest room, where I am to eat the passover with my disciples?' and he will show you a large upper room furnished; there make ready".' (Lk 22:8-12)

There was instruction in detail. In the setting, what poverty! The homeless Lord had to seek the hospitality of a poor man to celebrate the pasch. But the house was furnished and ready, with love in the hearts of those who would celebrate the institution of the Eucharist.

The more we reflect on the care and beauty of the divine preparation for that solemn event, the more we will want to make ready a furnishing of our hearts with faith and love, when we come for the celebration of the Eucharist.

And when the hour came, he sat at table,
and the apostles with him. (Lk 22:14)

Lord, make my heart ready and worthy to receive you.

Gift From His Heart

A gift can express a language, it can convey a message. We often express our esteem for a person by offering a gift; and for someone who ranks high in our affection, we try to choose a gift of special value.

When Jesus wished to express his limitless love of us he, too, chose a gift; not just a keepsake or souvenir, but nothing less than the gift of himself. No greater love than laying down his life for us, his friends; no greater gift than the Eucharist, given to us in that moment of supreme loving.

At the Last Supper, his love, like a river in flood, knew no bounds. He revealed the riches of his eucharistic heart as he offered to every person, and for all time, the gift of his Body and Blood, under sacramental signs of bread and wine.

When his side was opened on the Cross he revealed his heart open to receive and to give treasures beyond all imagining.

'Who,' said Pope Pius XII, 'can adequately depict the throbbings of his divine heart, tokens of his boundless love, at those precious moments when he bestowed his greatest gifts to mankind, that is to say, the gift of himself in the sacrament of the Eucharist?'

His giving is without limits. Shall we not give thanks without ceasing?

Take, eat, this is my body. (Mt 26:26)

Lord Jesus, keep me ever thanking you for your gift of the Eucharist.

Giving Thanks

The interior walls of the Rosary Basilica in Lourdes are lined with granite blocks. And on each is inscribed just one word, 'Thanks', with the name of the donor and the favour received. The walls themselves speak a massive expression of thanks.

Right through his life Jesus was constantly giving thanks to his Father.He thanked him for revealing to the little ones the secrets of his love. On the mountains by night he was united with his Father in a great prayer of praising and pleading. At the Last Supper, taking bread, he gave thanks. His sacrifice of his life was his supreme act of thanksgiving,by which he became our Eucharist.

The apostles gave faithful witness to the importance of thanksgiving. 'In everything by prayer and supplication with thanksgiving let your requests be made known to God.' (Eph 4:6)

Our world needs to learn the art of thanksgiving. There is more emphasis on having than on giving. G. K.Chesterton described St Francis of Assisi: 'He was above all things a great giver, and he cared chiefly for the best kind of giving which is called thanksgiving.'

It is for us to keep the prayer of thanksgiving in the forefront of our approach to our heavenly Father.

I thank my God in all my remembrance of you. (Phil 1:3)

Lord Jesus, teach me how to thank you with all my heart for all your favours, and make me grateful to all who deserve my thanks.

God Exists – I Have Met Him.

André Frossard wrote an absorbing book with the title *God exists. I have met him.* Behind the title lies a remarkable story of a journey from unbelief to faith. André described himself as 'a complacent atheist.'

He had a varied career: Naval officer, prisoner of the Gestapo for a year, when released, engaged as a journalist.

His remarkable story goes as follows. One evening he went for a drive with a friend, Willemin, a devout Catholic, along the Latin Quarter of Paris. Willemin went to visit a church which later he knew was a convent of Sisters of Perpetual Adoration.

After a while, out of curiosity, André followed in, He entered a chapel and, on an altar brightly lit, he saw a monstrance in which there was a host. Suddenly, looking on the host he was surrounded by a dense brilliant light. He tried to describe it: 'an avalanche descended upon me'. He saw reality; he saw truth. 'I was quite unaware that before me was the Blessed Sacrament below which many candles were burning.'

After he had been prepared for baptism by a priest of the Holy Ghost Order he was able to express his awareness of the full marvel of the Eucharist:

'I was amazed that the love of God should have used such an astonishing means of communication, and that for it bread, the food of the poor and of small children, had been God's choice. Of all the gifts which Christianity was showering upon me, the Eucharist seemed to me the greatest.'

Here is a story with a message for each of us. Reflecting on the experience of André Frossard we may, with an ever lively faith, say with St Thomas Aquinas, 'O Jesus, whom veiled I now behold, I beg you, that beholding you with countenance unveiled, I may be happy in the vision of your glory.'

I am the living bread which came down from heaven. (Jn 6:51)
Blessed be Jesus in the most holy sacrament of the altar.

God's Masterpiece

In the centre of a Roman Piazza there is a high column on top of which is a statue of Our Lady. It was erected to mark the occasion of the declaration in 1854 of the dogma of her Immaculate Conception.

Roman families come and place bouquets of white flowers around the base of the shrine on the feast day, so that by evening, the whole Piazza is one huge mass of white.

When Bezalel was commissiond to make the tabernacle, he was directed to use the most precious materials, acacia wood, silver and gold. It was 'lined with pure gold, within and without'. (Ex 37:9)

But there would be a tabernacle far more splendid. It was Mary, fashioned by the divine craftsman, to be a tabernacle for a Son. She would be adorned, within and without, with pure gold. And when the work was done, she was the masterpiece whose beauty no human words could describe, for she was 'tota pulchra', 'all fair'.

Her feast is the dawn breaking on the heights, preparing us for the birth of Jesus, Light of the World.

The sun plays equally on the muddy swamps as on the garden of flowers. Thus, her sinless beauty inspires the pure of heart to open out to God's love, like flowers before the sun, while, at the same time, it restores the sinful and despairing, telling them that a sinless mother intercedes for them with her son whom she gave to the world to take sin away.

Her beauty is out of this world. Her Immaculate Conception was given for our sake also, to lift us out of this world to make us fit tabernacles in which God would dwell.

He who is mighty has done great things for me. (Lk 1:49)

O Mary, conceived without sin, pray for us who have recourse to thee.

He Sat Down

To be seated is a posture that has many benefits. It gives relaxation, it can ease tension, it can relieve fatigue. To invite a visitor to be seated is a gesture of friendship. It expresses equality. It makes for that easy, genial conversation between friends, as person to person.

In varied gospel moments we find Jesus seated. 'He came again to the temple; all the people came to him, and he sat down and taught them.' (Jn 8:2) By sitting down he put them at their ease. He did not speak down to them from on high.

When the crowd were with him on the hillside he bade them sit down. He relieved their weariness and fed them. On another occasion, 'wearied as he was with his journey, he sat down by the well'. (Jn 4:6)

Something in his weariness touches us, and brings us closer to him. Fr Louis Bouyer aptly illustrated the idea: 'Perhaps it is more moving to see him subjected to the daily troubles which form the course of our daily, fallen existence, such as this weariness after a long tramp in the sun on a dusty road, than to know he is capable of suffering immense pain.'

With great delight I sat in his shadow. (Song 2:3)

*Lord, make me worthy to sit with you at the table of the Eucharist,
and in your eucharistic presence, in your shadow,
may I find delight and be constantly refreshed.*

He Was Wounded

The words of the prophet introduce us to the pathos of the sacred Passion of Jesus: 'And if anyone ask him, "What are these wounds on your back?" he will say, "The wounds I received in the house of my friends".' (Zech 13:6)

Every person, to the end of time, must ask the question, because it tells of him who carried the burden of all the sin of the world, and the marks of that burden are written on his body. The stripes on the body of Jesus open up a vision of boundless love proved by limitless suffering.

Why these wounds? The prophet explains, 'He was wounded for our transgressions, he was bruised for our iniquities ... with his stripes we are healed.' (Is 53:5) The stripes that marked him are the stripes that healed us.

St Bernard describes his wounds as a treasure for us; they are 'like honey from the rock', from the wounds of his sacred passion, a key that opens the gateway to his heart. Jesus was wounded by love; he loves by being wounded.

Can we, even in a small way, repay him for the wounds he endured out of love, by accepting with patience and love the hurts and wounds which we may sustain?

The risen Jesus allowed his wounds to be touched in order to strengthen faith in the reality of his victory over death and sin. He deepens our love when, with tenderness, we try to dress the wounds of his people. An Eastern writer reminds us: 'Since my Ascension, you can touch my pierced hands and my open side, only if you bend down in compassion over the wounds of men. My living presence will become certain for you in this contact with the suffering members of my Body.'

Your wounds I will heal. (Jer 30:17)

Heart of Jesus, wounded for our sins, have mercy on us.

Heart For The Crowd

Like a tidal wave of humanity, a 'great throng' surged towards Jesus, a flotsam and jetsam of life, bringing their sick to him. There was a sense of urgency about their coming. 'They followed him on foot from the towns.' (Mt 14:13)

He did not turn away from them. He had compassion on them. (Mt 14:14) His look penetrated; he saw the crises behind their eyes; his love went out to them to ease their burdens. 'He healed their sick.'

Through the Church Jesus continues his healing mission in our time. Do we not find the gospel scene accurately interpreted by the opening words of the Second Vatican Council's *Pastoral Constitution on the Church in the Modern World?* 'The joys and the hopes, the griefs and anxieties of the men of our age, especially those who are poor or in any way afflicted, these are the joys and hopes, the griefs and anxieties of the followers of Christ.' They are 'the great throng' on the pilgrim road, some singing, some weeping, some 'buffeted between hope and anxiety, some burdened with uneasiness.'

The Church interprets these 'signs of the times' in the light of the gospel. All of us can be messengers of the compassion of Jesus to those around us who may be burdened.

He will have compassion according to the abundance of his steadfast love. (Lam 3:33)

Lord, open my heart with compassion for those in need.

Immediately

Sometimes life runs smoothly; sometimes interrupted by a sudden problem or crisis. We have to try to cope with it immediately.

That word 'immediately' keeps recurring through the gospel. It is centred on an urgent cry for help in a sudden crisis. It describes a coming to the rescue. The response of Jesus is always immediate.

To men in a small boat, struggling against a strong tide, he came. 'Immediately he spoke to them and said, "Take heart, it is I, have no fear".' (Mk 6:50)

A woman touched his garment, and 'immediately the haemorrhage ceased.' (Mk 5:29)

Jesus responds immediately to the pleading of a blind man for sight.

In our lives the word 'immediately' can step out of the gospel pages as Jesus comes to our rescue.

How often a crisis hits us – an urgent problem, a grave illness, a deep disappointment – and we cry out, 'Come, Lord, and help me.' And we find that our cry from the heart reaches his heart. Immediately he comes to our aid.

Life can be a voyage in calm waters. But sometimes we are caught, like a craft in a dark night in a dangerous storm. What relief when Jesus comes immediately, walking on the waters, as to the apostles, to reassure us!

And immediately he received his sight. (Mk 10:52)

Lord, come quickly to help me when I am in trouble.
Give a helping hand to all who need you.

In The Palm Of His Hand

A woman from Arizona whose husband had died, felt overpowered by loneliness. She decided to go to live to New York, where she felt she would find companionship. But she found that in the presence of millions she was still alone.

One day when reading through scripture she came across a phrase: 'God, in whom we live and move and have our being.' (Acts 17:26) That consoling thought settled her down. God, holding her in the palm of his hand, gave her an overpowering sense of his protective presence.From then on, she would never be less alone than when alone.

There are many people in the world like her, and for them, I present, with love, a few thoughts, in verse form.

Stay by my side, O Lord, for I'm alone.
I need your presence with me,
Night and day, to share my home,
To guide me on my way.

Keep me safe from danger,
Fill my heart with joy,
Give me your peace, your gift,
To share with those whose hearts
Are troubled or despair.

And even when the shadow
Of the cross falls on my path,
I see your Easter sunlight
Through the dark.

I live alone, dear Lord,
But I am sure
Your gaze is ever on me,
As on an only child.

Abide in me, dear Lord,
That I may live in you. Amen.

I am with you always. (Mt 28:20)

Into Galilee

A person who has been through a grave trial or depression often re-cives medical advice to get away for a rest to some quiet place.

Within a few hours the apostles underwent the gravest shock of their lives. When Jesus was taken in Gethsemane 'All the disciples forsook him and ran away.' (Mt 6:56) And there was worse to come. There was Calvary. On Easter day 'the doors being shut where the disciples were for fear of the Jews'. (Jn 20:19) They were men haggard, drained of courage.

And then the message came from two angelic figures at the tomb through Mary Magdalene and the women: 'Go tell his disciples and Peter that he is going before you into Galilee; there you will see him.' (Mk 16:7)

There in the calm of those lovely sunrises on the lake, in the presence of happy memories of the call, of seedtime and harvest, of lilies in bloom, the risen Jesus came to them, bringing the freshness of springtime of a new world.

There is something for all of us in that story of the risen Jesus in Galilee. Each one of us at some time has had our Gethsemane or Calvary, an ordeal too hard to bear – a project failure; leaving us desolate with our blighted hopes. In such moments there is a Galilee we need. An expert on the gospels has recaptured the beauty of that moment.

'He will go before you into Galilee ... "My child, I shall be faithful to the appointment which I made with you. I shall do more than wait for you in this Galilee of memories. I shall lead you there. When your heart is once again fixed on Galilee, the one who is guiding you will make himself known to you, and he will seek you ...".'

Jesus said to the women, 'Go and tell my brethren to go to Galilee, and there they will see me.' (Mt 28:10)

Lord, put into my heart the calm and peace of Galilee.
Give rest and courage to all troubled hearts.

Just An Echo And A Fragrance

Monsignor Ronald Knox uses a telling phrase to describe Mary: 'In most of Our Lord's life-history her name is scarcely more than an echo and a fragrance.

An echo: Her first words spoken in the silence of the hills. As she travelled the hill country her feet made no noise. Once only her voice was raised in a canticle of song to the Lord who had done great things in her.

In her finest hour we read simply that she stood. There, those words which contain the central message of her life echoed in her heart, and united her with the thoughts that were uppermost in the heart of her son in that moment. Again, Knox's words: 'All Calvary is eloquent with the throbbing of her unspoken prayer.'

Words unspoken, but echoing a message relevant to all of us. *'Fiat.'* 'Let it be to me according to your word.' (Lk 1:38) It is for us to unite with the will of her son at that moment. 'They have no wine.' (Jn 2:3) Now, as at Cana, she presents to him our need for the wine of salvation. 'Do whatever he tells you.' (Lk 2:5) Those were her last spoken words. Famous last words that are meant to echo into every human heart, and family and nation till the end of time.

A fragrance: Mary walked, almost unseen, unnoticed, just a woman in the crowd. But she remains the *'Rosa Mystica'* the hidden rose, little in stature, but with a fragrance that spreads abroad. A writer has said: 'The rose draws people to itself and the scent remains with them. A rose does not preach. It simply spreads its fragrance by being there.'

Could we ask her to keep her gospel message echoing in our minds, and the fragrance of her holiness to purify our hearts?

But Mary kept all these things, pondering them in her heart.
(Lk 2:19)

Mary, keep your words ever echoing in my heart,
so that I may make my life a fragrant offering to the Lord.

Just As I Am

Jean Vanier tells how deeply he was moved by the words of a young boy, severly handicapped, who said to him: 'Jesus loves me just as I am.'

With speech impaired, and movement limited, but his heart in perfect health, he was capable of that simple childlike thought that was a perfect prayer, which must have won a special response from the heart of Jesus.

Those words of his describe the kind of way that Jesus loves, and the kind of person to whom his heart goes out.

Right through the gospel pages we find Jesus meeting and loving people just as they were, seemingly casually, taking them by surprise. Zacchaeus, handicapped in size, a woman who had been taken in adultery, a blind man just sitting on the roadside, a child taken in his arms.

So does he take us, just as we are, in our working clothes, with all our virtues and defects, successes and failures. Just in the here and now he finds us and accepts us.

That young boy with Jean Vanier preached to us a gospel within a gospel, a way of childlike faith and humility, of openness of heart.

In whatever state or moment he finds me, he loves me just as I am.

And Jesus, looking upon him, loved him. (Mk 10:21)

Lord, I beg you to accept me just as I am.

Lest We Forget

When we receive an important message, very often, lest we forget, we put it in writing.

In the Book of Deuteronomy an important message is given to us. We are asked to 'Hear', to give it our full attention, and write it in our hearts. 'Hear, O Israel, the precepts of the Lord, and write them in your hearts as in a book; and I will give you a land flowing with milk and honey.' (Deut.4:1, 6:9)

These commandments of the Lord deserve our full attention, for they have to do with the whole area of our behaviour that ultimately can win us reward.

Pope John Paul II describes the moment in the gospel when the young man came to Jesus asking the question, 'Teacher, what good must I do to have eternal life?' and received the reply, 'Keep the commandments.' (Mt 16:17)

'We allow ourselves to be guided by Jesus' reply, allowing ourselves to be guided by him. Jesus, as a patient and sensitive teacher, answers the young man by taking him, as it were, by the hand, and leading him step by step to the full truth.' *(Veritatis Splendor)*

So does he lead us, step by step.

If you would enter into life, keep the commandments. (Mt 19:17)

Lord, help me to grow in your love by keeping your commandments.
Lead us to love your law.

Like A Rose Planted

Over the entrance to the Rosary Basilica in Lourdes are inscribed the words 'Like a rose planted by the rivers of water, bear fruit'.

They form a fitting background for a reflection on the message of Lourdes. 'Like a rose' – without movement a rose transmits its own fragrance. By its beauty of colour and richness of scent, it draws people in admiration.

When the Immaculate Virgin appeared, two roses in full bloom were at her feet. Mary is titled the 'Mystical Rose', the 'Hidden Rose', and by her very presence she transformed a fetid refuse dump with a fragrance that has, ever since, filled the grotto.

That fragrance drew and filled the heart of the little girl who knelt at her feet. It is said that 'the person who is loved, generates love'. Bernadette was loved with the tender love of a mother. Just as the beauty of the Lady was reflected on her countenance, so her soul was enriched. She generated love. She grew in holiness like a rose in full bloom, and the fragrance of her holiness has been transmitted to countless souls.

'Planted by the rivers of water.' The prophet described the grace of salvation: 'Waters shall break forth in the wilderness.' (Is 35:7) At the word of the Virgin waters sprang up from the earth, at first a trickle, but growing into a mighty river, a great sacramental fountain.

'Bear fruit.' From that source unending, what a fruitful gain! An unending song of praise and pleading, a cleansing from sin, a feeding with the Bread of Life, a comforting and easing of the burden of suffering.

'Like a rose planted' is more than a colourful phrase. It describes the reality of holiness, that has been the experience, like the beauty of a rose,that has entranced countless human hearts.

The desert shall rejoice and blossom. (Is 35:1)

Our Lady of Lourdes, pray for me.

Limping Across A Battlefield

During the Korean war a photo appeared in American newspapers of a little Korean girl walking through the ruins of a village, seen in the background. She was limping, with a stick, her head covered in bandages, and tears streaming down her cheeks. She was an orphan of war. Within days, letters began arriving at the State Department in Washington from families offering to take the little girl into their home.

A touching story of compassion. Those people's hearts were touched by the condition and suffering of that little girl.

That child's plight reminds us that, in a sense, we are all limping across the battlefield, needing the bandage of compassion. None of us but has been wounded by sin. But that war weary child opens our eyes all the more vividly to the love of the heart of Jesus for us. 'He was wounded for our transgressions, he was bruised for our iniquities.' (Is 53:5)

He looks on us with compassion. He bends down to lift the fallen. His love comes immediately to our rescue. We are no longer abandoned victims on a battlefield. His heart, open to restore us, challenges our hearts.

So we are capable of making our own the prayer of St Paul:

'Blessed be the God and Father of our Lord Jesus Christ, the Father of mercies and God of all comfort, who comforts us in all our afflictions, so that we may be able to comfort those who are in any affliction, with the comfort with which we ourselves are comforted by God.' (2 Cor 1:3, 4)

He heals the brokenhearted, and binds up their wounds.
(Ps 147:3)

Lord, lift me when I fall, and heal the pain of those who suffer.

Looking Towards Him

We tend instinctively to turn our eyes away from a scene of horror, from a graphic picture of violence. Sometimes before a TV programme is shown, the presenter announces, 'Viewers may find some of the scenes in this programme disturbing.'

But there is one scene of horror which we are invited not to turn away from, but to look full upon. It is the figure of Jesus crucified, his sacred countenance disfigured almost beyond recognition, his body torn with lashes, extended on the cross.

The prophet put into words an urgent cry from the heart of the dying Saviour: 'All you who pass by the way, attend and see if there be any sorrow like to my sorrow.' (Lam 1:12)

We are invited to look, not with a casual glance, but to 'attend', to come close and give our full attention to him as he was dying, an innocent victim for the world's sin. Never would there be such sorrow.

St John rounds off his account of Calvary with the words of the prophet: 'They shall look on him whom they have pierced.' (Jn 19:37) A looking that is focused, attentive with the eyes of the heart. Love has eyes, and we cannot fail to look on him with love.

'One of the soldiers pierced his side with a lance.' (Jn 19:34) St Bonaventure describes that action: 'They pierced with the lance of rage his holy heart, which had long been wounded by the lance of love.' It was the opening of a window that allowed us to look on the entrancing beauty of the vision of his heart.

His side was pierced. His heart was opened. Let us look!

He was a man of sorrows, and acquainted with grief. (Is 53:3)

We adore you, O Christ, and praise you,
because by your holy Cross you have redeemed the world.

Love And Betrayal

Great writers and composers have portrayed the tragic experience of love given, which, instead of response, suffers betrayal.

On the night of the supreme revelation of his love, Jesus suffered betrayal. 'On the night he was betrayed, he took bread ...'

We are so familiar with those words that they tend to pass over our heads. The night began at the table, when Jesus revealed his heart bursting with intense love: 'I have earnestly desired to eat this passover with you before I suffer.' (Lk 22:15) His love, like a river bursting its banks, so overflowed on that night that, for the moment, he pushed the thought of his impending passion into the background.

One version of the phrase goes, 'With desire I have desired', conveying the idea of deepest longing. St Augustine says 'desire' is itself prayer. Here it was a prayer of intense longing of Jesus to give himself.

On the Cross, he would again express his desire: 'I thirst' – from his heart, a corresponding longing to receive, to be loved.

At the supper love reached its summit. No greater love than to give up his life in sacrifice. 'This is my body which will be given up for you.' For all time, the table has become the altar of sacrifice.

And for all time, from that altar, he would be given back, his supreme gift to us. 'Take, all of you and eat.' What is our response? Surely, to give ourselves totally to him, to return love for love.

Do this in remembrance of me. (Lk 22:19)

Lord, You are the Bread come down from heaven.
You are the food of life eternal.

Love That Conquers

In every age there has been a variety of ways of inflicting suffering.

Writing to the Romans St Paul listed what he had to endure – distress, beatings, false brethren, sleepless nights, danger from robbers, shipwreck. What a litany of trials! Any one of them would have been beyond our endurance. But Paul could take them in his stride.

Why? They were endured by a man who was on fire with love of Christ. Once he had made the love of Christ his own he possessed a reckless energy, an unbounded enthusiasm, that made him feel a conquerer … 'through him who loved us'.

He was very conscious of having been chosen and his one aim in life was to return something of the love which Christ showed him, and to preach the inexhaustible riches of Christ to the whole world.

Love desires union, and to ensure that this union would be unbroken, he wished to feel nailed with Christ to the Cross.

For Paul there could be only one real tragedy – to be separated from Christ.

His example gives us courage. He strengthens our conviction, that we try to ensure that for us also nothing should separate us from the love of Christ.

Who shall separate us from the love of Christ? (Rom 8:15)

Lord Jesus, help us, after the example of St Paul,
to grow and rejoice in your love.

Love Travels

A ship in distress sends out a mayday signal for help. Immediately there is a response by sea and air.

So does love travel. The person who loves responds, as to a mayday signal, to the need of a friend in need of help. Sometimes it may be to share a burden, or to share an experience of joy.

Mary's response of love to her cousin's need was to rise up. 'She went with haste.' (Lk 1:39) St Ambrose reminds us that 'she went with haste not with hurry'. Her going was not a fretful, anxious rushing. It was a journey with composure, with a sense of urgency. Her love travelled.

When shepherds heard of the birth of the Saviour, 'they went with haste'. (Lk 12:16)

Magdelene's love of her Lord made her run to the tomb. 'She ran and went to Simon Peter and the other disciple ... they both ran.' (Jn 20:2, 4)

We can learn from those gospel moments to go with haste to help our neighbour as did Mary, and to share with shepherds and Magdalene the joy of the coming and rising of the Lord.

And Mary remained with her about three months. (Lk 1:56)

*Lord Jesus, help us to learn from the gospel how love travels,
and how to make us respond to need.*

Love Unloved

A hymn for the Feast of the Sacred Heart of Jesus has a verse:
> Who will not love in return the one who loves him?
> Who, being redeemed, will not love his Redeemer?

Only love can respond to love. The love of Jesus for us is boundless in time and space and, therefore, all the more deserves a generous response of gratitude.

A gospel moment presents the experience of gratitude and ingratitude. Ten men suffering from the dread disease of leprosy cried out to Jesus for mercy and immediately he cured them. His love reached out to touch the untouchable.

They had been quick to plead but slow to thank. They went their way without a word, all but one who returned. And with a heart overflowing with gratitude, he fell on his face at Jesus' feet, giving him thanks. Jesus said, 'Were not ten cleansed? Where are the nine?' (Lk 17:16, 17)

Down the corridors of time the Heart of Jesus continues to go out to heal, to redeem, to comfort, and he still meets ingratitude. Where are the nine?

Revealing his love to St Margaret Mary, he makes the plaintive cry: 'Behold this heart which has loved men so much, but is loved so little in return.'

We all need to behold his Heart, and to ask ourselves: 'What return shall I render to the Lord for all his goodness to me?' (Ps 115:12)

She tells us how to respond: 'O my God, I offer you your beloved Son, in thanksgiving for all your goodness to me. I offer him as my adoration, my petition, my oblation, my resolutions. I offer him as my love and my all.'

Let us not allow love to go unloved.

Sing to the Lord, giving thanks. (Ps 146:7)

Lord, teach us to be generous in responding to your love.

Mass At The Centre

A young Christian community at Abiteme, in the early church, was assembled for the Sunday celebration of the Eucharist when an edict came from the emperor that the celebration was forbidden. And a cry went up from the whole assembly: 'But we cannot live without the Eucharist!'

Across the span of the centuries is a parallel.

A priest from Prague with whom I shared the joy of Ordination to the priesthood at the same time in Rome, was sentenced to twenty-five years' imprisonment because of his apostolate as a priest. After twenty-two years in prison he was released on condition that he would work in a state factory, but never as a priest. After work, at a kitchen table in a basement flat, with a a piece of bread and a cup of wine, he celebrated Mass. Asked if he was ever tempted to give up his faith, he replied, 'As long as I have the Mass I feel I have something to offer to the Church in my country.'

Both those histories exemplify the conviction of the Eucharist as the 'centre and summit of the Christian life'. They inspire us to keep strong the same conviction.

If any one eats this bread, he will live for ever. (Jn 6:51)

Lord Jesus, strengthen my faith,
so that I may keep the Mass at the centre of my life.

Message In Marble

There is a famous cemetery at Staglieno, near Genoa, where back along the years Genovese families had their family tombs adorned with great columns of white marble, on which were often depicted scenes from the gospel.

One of them shows the raising of the daughter of Jairus, with Jesus standing by the bedside of the little girl. His one hand takes her by the hand, and his other hand points upwards to the skies. Thus the artist vividly presents the interplay of the human and divine in Jesus.

The heart of Jesus was moved by the urgent pleading of the little girl's father: 'Come and lay your hands on her, that she may be made well and live.' (Mk 5:23) 'Taking her by the hand, Jesus said to her "Little girl, I say to you arise", and immediately she got up.' (Mk 5:41) He exercised his divine power. 'He told them to give her something to eat.' (Mk 5:43)

Here is his human concern.

The only witnesses were her parents and Peter, James and John, who shortly afterwards would see him in the glory of Tabor, and, later, would need both those memories to strengthen them against the scandal of the Cross.

At any time we can place ourselves in that room, and be filled with amazement and find, in the words and actions of Jesus, encouragement and joy.

On the day I called you answered me. (Ps 137:3)

Lord Jesus, in crisis moments of my life, I rush to you.
Come to me as you came in the gospel,
and teach me the unforgettable experience
of the divine and human in you.

Moments Of Decision

There are moments and decisions in life which call for preparation

In the public ministry of Jesus there were events and decisions closely related to the whole plan of salvation. The gospels tell us how he brought his prayer specifically to bear on such events.

He is praying before choosing his apostles. He is praying alone before setting out on his teaching mission. Before the storm at sea he prays – he would be strengthening their faith. Before the Transfiguration he ascended the mountain to pray.

Before Peter's profession of faith Jesus prayed, as again later he prayed for Peter: 'I have prayed for you that your faith may not fail.' (Lk 22:31)

All this was within the setting of his prayer which was a constant, whether on the mountain or on crowded roads.

In our lives there are events central to our salvation – our celebration of the Eucharist, sacrifice and sacrament, the sacrament of Penance. The example of Jesus can help us to prepare for them with prayer.

There may occur a moment which is a test of faith, when we would call on Jesus to pray for us that our faith might not fail. One of those unexpected storms may strike us, when we would pray him to restore our courage as he did for the apostles.

And when it was night he continued in prayer to God.
And when it was day, he called his apostles. (Lk 6:12, 13)

Lord, help me to prepare worthily for the sacraments;
keep my faith firm and my courage strong.

Morning Has Broken

Along the eastern horizon appear a few streaks of light, and the curtain of night begins to lift. Morning has broken and a new day has begun, and with it the promise of another moment of life, a sign of hope.

Our waking moments differ. Sometimes we start off refreshed after peaceful sleep. Sometimes the burden of living is back with us as we start a new day. The day ahead is a test of faith or hope. How can we face a day like yesterday?

It is reassuring for us to recall where Jesus so often spent those hours before dawn. 'A great while before day, he rose and went out to a lonely place and there he prayed.' (Mk 1:35) He had been awake before the world awoke to a new dawn, and already in prayer for it.

Thus he remains, present in all our dawns.

The apostles found him to tell him, 'Every one is searching for you.' (Mk 1:37) The phrase almost conveys the idea of their forming a queue, to present to him their thanks and their pleadings.

So we take our place in the queue, certain that Jesus listens to each of us, and to reassure us that he will be with us in every moment of the coming day.

In the morning, O Lord, you hear my voice. (Ps 5:3)

Lord Jesus, I place this new day in your hands,
and may I carry your love to all who cross my path today.

My Eyes And My Heart

Twice the Lord expressed to Solomon his plan for the completion of the temple, and on each occasion, he made a promise.

'I have consecrated this house which you have built, and put my name there for ever; my eyes and my heart will be there for ever.' (1 Kings 9:3) And on another occasion he promised: 'Now my eyes will be open and my ears attentive to the prayer that is made in this place.' (2 Chron 7:15)

The beauty and the message of those words can enrich our awareness of the presence of Jesus in the Blessed Sacrament, and of the power which his presence brings.

Your eyes are there. As I come into your presence, how better can I begin than by asking you to look, as you did in the gospel. Your one glance was enough to draw hearts, and to melt them to tears.

You turned and looked on Andrew and his companion, and drew them to become your disciples. You looked on Peter and wept. Your heart is there, loving, consoling, refreshing the weary, and bestowing peace.

Your ears are attentive to all those plaintive cries for help, for those whispered pleadings, for generous words of thanks.

For your looking, for your listening, and for your loving, my unending thanks.

To live through love in his presence. (Eph 1:4)

Lord Jesus, increase my awareness of your presence in the holy Eucharist.

O Saving Victim

St Thomas Aquinas had the gift of presenting in short words the mystery of the holy Eucharist. Here is a stanza of one of his eucharistic poems:

O Saving victim, opening wide
The gates of heaven to men below.
Our foes press on from every side,
Thine aid, supply, thy strength bestow.

To reflect on it, line by line, is to enrich our response of love of Jesus in the Eucharist.

The Victim: We recall his supreme sacrificial love offering, becoming a victim, offering his life for us. 'Christ loved us, and gave himself up for us, a fragrant offering and sacrifice to God.' (Eph 5:2)

The Saviour: Coming into this world he was greeted as Saviour. 'For you is born this day in the city of David, a Saviour.' (Lk 2:11) He saved us at the expense of total giving, and now he continues to give himself – each day he is present to us as Saviour in his sacramental presence.

The open gates: Inviting us here to share in the eucharistic celebration, he gives us a pledge of future glory.

The Request: We plead for strength to overcome the fatigue of our pilgrim journey, for refreshment in hope.

We need his help in all those crises, great or small, which we encounter on the road of life.

I am with you always, to the close of the age. (Mt 28:20)

Blessed be Jesus in the most holy sacrament of the altar.

On Every Road

There is a picture of a wayside Calvary shrine in France. It is placed at the bend of a road, and beneath it the words, 'Christ is there on every road.'

Both the picture and the words present a very comforting message: that, at every step of our pilgrim road, at every bend, Christ is there with us as our fellow traveller.

Turning over the gospel pages we find him so often on the road. At one moment he is on the road to exile; at another, crossing sun baked hills, from town to town, or standing on the road awaiting the crowd eagerly rushing towards him. On his final journey to Jerusalem, the shadow of the cross was on the road as he approached.

The same pattern is verified in our day-to-day living as we travel the road. The same Lord is our companion and support. There can be unexpected road bends with unexpected turns of events that disturb our peace. Just as we may encounter poor visibility, there can be factors which cloud our sense of direction.

In such moments, we instinctively fall back on him who is The Way, to keep us unharmed, on the right path.

In paths that they have not known I will guide them. (Is 42:16)

Lord Jesus, I need your help at every step of my road;
stay near me and guide me.
To all travellers give a safe journey.

Only Say The Word

Lord, I am not worthy to receive you, but only say the word and I shall be healed. How many deep truths are condensed in those words! They are an expression of faith, an impulse of longing, a tribute of thanks.

We have heard them so often. Lest, through repetition, the marvel they express should be dimmed, we need, each time, as if hearing them for the first time, to refresh our sense of wonder at their revelation of the healing and saving love of Jesus.

To do this it is useful for us to bring the gospel scene, where those words were first spoken, on to the stage of memory.

On the stage, a little action-packed drama is taking place. A crisis, a matter of life and death, a deep stirring of faith in the heart of a man who is a soldier and pagan. His urgent cry for help. He addresses Jesus: 'Lord, my servant is lying paralysed at home, in terrible distress.' And he said to him: 'I will come and heal him.' But the centurion answered him, 'Lord, I am not worthy to have you come under my roof, but only say the word, and my servant will be healed.' (Mt 8:6-8)

Another account says he sent messengers. But in either version there is an example of astonishing faith. Jesus 'wondered at his faith', and paid him an effusive tribute: 'Truly, I say to you, not even in Israel have I found such faith.' (Mt 8:10)

St John Chrysostom explains why Jesus worked this miracle: 'He did this that we might learn the virtues of the centurion.'

As we approach the holy Eucharist could we be as eager to come to Jesus as he is to come to us? Shall we not also pray to him not only to heal and restore us, but to transform us through the Eucharist, into his own likeness?

Sir, come down before my child dies (Jn 4:49).

Lord Jesus, make me every more worthy to receive you,
and to make for you a home in my heart.
Fill me with wonder at your gift of the holy Eucharist.

Our Lady Of Knock

Mother love is special. It is a love that is tender and reckless, ready to endure the gravest hazard to rescue a child in danger. None of us could have survived without it.

Mary is the perfect mother. She exercised motherhood of her son, serving him in his person and in his work. At Calvary she stood beneath the cross. In lonely grandeur she stood in silence.

Is not the history of Knock Shrine close to the drama of Calvary? On the altar is the Lamb, offering himself to take away the sins of the world. And in that offering Mary is united with him. As his side was opened, her heart was pierced. Two hearts, one love.

And in that moment she received a new spiritual motherhood. The exchange that took place at Calvary is ever being renewed, and visibly recalled at the altar at Knock. Mary received John, and all of us, in a new maternal embrace. And we, like John, are ever being invited to behold our mother.

The presence of Joseph recognises his unique mission as guardian of the Church.

Preaching at Mass at Knock Shrine, Pope John Paul II, addressing Mary, said: 'In this shrine you gather the People of God of all Ireland, and constantly point out to them Christ in the Eucharist and in the Church.'

When we come here we can make our own his words of consecration to Mary: 'We entrust and consecrate to you, Mother of Christ and Mother of the Church, our hearts, our consciences, our works.'

Our hearts: to be drawn to her Immaculate Heart, and presented to her Son. *Our consciences:* open to the truth of the gospel, to discern good from evil. *Our works:* the day to day living of our Christian life in line with our faith.

Do whatever he tells you. (Jn 2:5)

Our Lady of Knock, pray for us.

Over The Hills And Far Away

In a radio competition a prize was offered to one who would suggest the most descriptive phrase in the English language. The prize winner was 'Over the hills and far away'.

That lovely phrase portrays a sense of mystery, a picture of an undulating roll of hills, winding away into the great beyond, the journey towards eternity,

The traveller reaches the top of one hill, and there before him lies another, maybe higher, and then perhaps a ridge of mountains farther on. On the ascent, perhaps a ledge of level ground, a stopping place, from where he looks upwards, thinking he is near the top. But the summit is not yet.

St Gregory of Nyssa fills in the picture: 'Each peak we strive for fills our entire horizon, and then when we reach it, another rises up.'

Doesn't the picture somehow come near describing our Christian journey through life? Isn't life just like that – the day-to-day struggle, the test of endurance, like a strenuous hill climb. As we mount one hill, another opens out before us. A moment of decision about an important project, the start of the road of marriage, the beginning of a new journey following the call to the priesthood or religious life. The great adventure over the hills towards a destination far ahead.

A daunting adventure into the unknown, but not quite unknown or unaccompanied, for the psalm gives us a song for the road, as well as an assurance that we do not walk alone: 'I lift my eyes to the hills, from whence does my help come? My help comes from the Lord.' (Ps 121:1, 2)

The Lord your God is bringing you into a good land
… flowing forth in valleys and hills. (Deut 8:7)

Lord, grant me the grace to walk wih courage and hope
the road of life.
Give a safe journey to all travellers.

Perchance To Dream

Could a dream come true? A memory of a lovely past again become a reality? A prospect of a sunlit future, is it fantasy or reality? Perchance to dream! These have been themes of great novels and of dramatic music.

But they are also at the heart of the great drama of salvation. God's people in exile, living under unbearable burdens, wondered if they would ever again be on the road to freedom. Would the long night ever end?

And then, the divine intervention. A loving God brings about their deliverance from bondage. Could it be true? It seemed like a dream.

'When the Lord delivered Sion from bondage, it seemed like a dream. Then was our mouth filled with laughter, on our lips there were songs.' (Ps 125:1) A people freed burst out into a song of thanks. 'What marvels the Lord worked for us. Indeed we were glad.' (Ps 125:3)

Even the heathens were puzzled. 'The heathens themselves said: "What marvels the Lord worked for them!" '

For each of us, that history keeps repeating. In our moments of trial when deliverance seems so far away, it seems like a dream. But the same loving God, through his intimate love for us, makes our dream a reality. Indeed we are glad!

O God, make haste to my rescue. Lord, come to my aid. (Ps 69:1)

Lord, with thanks for your loving care,
I trust in your help to free me from the trials of life.
Ease the burdens of those who are heavy laden.

Places To Remember

There are places which call up memories. They can be related to the setting in which important events in our lives took place.

In the gospel, Jesus chose places to convey his teaching. St Ambrose calls our attention to three such places:

The desert, to present the battle against sin.

A field of corn, to preach the kingdom.

A garden, where to experience his agony.

The desert: 'Jesus was led up by the Spirit to be tempted by the devil.' (Mt 4:1) Three times he did battle, and each time he overcame. Then the devil left him.

A field of corn: There was the seed time, and then the arrival of harvest, with fields ready for reaping. But there was a shortage of harvesters.So he appealed for prayer to the Lord of the harvest to send labourers to reap the harvest.

A garden: In the desert Jesus had been alone; but in Gethsemane, the place of his agony, he asked for companions: 'Stay here, and watch with me.' (Mt 26:39) And when he found them sleeping, he urged them to keep watching and praying lest they enter into temptation.

In each of the places there is an example of the centrality of prayer. There is a message for all of us of the power of prayer to overcome temptation, of the need of prayer that the harvest not be lost, the fruit of prayer that won the harvest of the Cross.

Watch and pray that you may not enter into temptation.
(Mt 26:4l)

Lord, help me to realise that in all my needs, by prayer I shall overcome.

Power In Showing Mercy

The power and beauty of God are all around us, flashing forth in his universe. The elements of water and fire express the immensity of his power. Stand on the cliffs of Moher and watch the grandeur of the sea, the power of those mighty breakers crashing against the cliffs.

How a forest fire can spread till almost beyond human control! In the tiniest item of his creation, in a primrose in a crannied wall, we can admire the marvel of his creative love, and a revelation still more marvellous – the unearthly radiance of a child's smile.

Still farther on we have the supreme proof of his almighty power, revealed in his showing mercy. The prayer of the Mass of the 26th Sunday of the year describes it: 'Father, you show your almighty power in your mercy and forgiveness.'

The Latin version has ... power 'above all' in showing mercy.

A whispered word, 'I absolve you,' in the sacrament of Penance and his infinite mercy restores and refreshes life.

We celebrate his love through our appreciation of his mercy, for mercy is love's second name.

He said to St Catherine of Siena: 'I can be recognised by mercy.' He wishes to be recognised by mercy in our generation, and we can be enriched in his merciful love by our use of the Sacrament of his mercy.

I trust in your merciful love. (Ps 12:5)

*Lord, help me to recognise your mercy
and to rejoice in your merciful love.*

Prayer Beyond Frontiers

An impressive feature of our time is the widening awareness of the world as a universal family, with crossing of colour bars, of political divides, with programmes for world health, poverty relief, world peace.

Before leaving this world Jesus presented a world programme: 'Go into the whole world, and preach the gospel to all creation.' (Mk 16:15) The Church has never lost sight of its universal mission.

The Second Vatican Council recalls the plan of the eternal Father: 'to dignify men with a participation in his own divine life. All those who would believe in Christ he planned to assemble in the holy church.' It lists those who have not yet received the gospel who are related in various ways to the People of God:

– the people from whom Christ was born in the flesh.

– those who acknowledge the Creator, among them, the Moslems, who along with us adore the one and merciful God.

– those who, through no fault of their own, do not know the gospel, yet sincerely seek God, strive to do his will.

– those who have not an explicit knowledge of God, but strive, aided by his grace, to lead a good life.

We ask the Holy Spirit to inspire us to think with the Church, and to pray with the Church, that our prayer without frontiers would extend to these four groups presented by the Council. *(Constitution on the Church)*

That they all may be one. (Jn 17:21)

Lord, open all human hearts to the grace of faith.

Rejected By His Own

The world's news brings repeated experiences of rejection. The fate of ethnic groups cut off from the community of a nation touches our hearts.

One scene early in the public life of Jesus must always cause a stirring in our hearts. It is described in details which highlight the trauma of rejection which he suffered. 'He came to Nazareth, where he had had been brought up.' (Lk 4:16) It would have seemed natural that he would receive welcome in his own home town.

Initially, 'the eyes of all in the Synagogue were fixed on him … and all spoke well of him.' (Lk 4:20, 22) But quickly the hearts of all in the synagogue closed against him and, in an outbreak of rage, they rushed him up to the brow of the hill, wishing to throw him down headlong. The drama closes with one short phrase: 'But passing through the midst of them he went away.' (Lk.4:30)

Zeferelli's film visually portrays that scene of tragic rejection. He depicts Jesus walking into the far distance through the olive groves, a solitary figure, walking alone, made homeless by his own.

A more terrible rejection would come, when Jesus on his way to Calvary, walking through the midst of them, went on his way to the Cross. There they had their way; they could lay hold of him to cast him down on the Cross.

Can we move through that story from beginning to conclusion, without being moved?

He was despised and rejected by men. (Is 52:3)

Lord, open my heart to give you welcome.
Comfort all who suffer rejection.

Remember Me

With his arms extended to embrace the whole world, with his limitless love infinitely available, the dying Jesus gave his final gesture of love to just one poor criminal dying beside him. For all time he gave proof of his personal care for every individual human soul. He who had compassion on the multitude has the same compassion on the one.

The dying man did not ask for a favour; he asked just to be remembered: 'Lord, remember me when you enter into your kingdom.' (Lk 23:42)

But even in his poverty he had something to offer. St Gregory explains: 'He believed in the future kingdom of the Lord whom he saw dying beside him . He had hope – that he would enter the kingdom. He had charity – he rebuked the other criminal, and explained to him that this man had done nothing wrong.'

One of the great French preachers has given us a perfect comment on the words of Jesus:

'Today' – What promptitude!

'With me' – What companionship!

'In paradise' – What reward!

A reflection that could occupy us for a lifetime.

He loved me and gave himself for me. (Gal 2:20)

*Lord, help me each day to remember with thanks
the love you gave me on the Cross,
so that in my final today
I may be worthy to enter into your kingdom.*

Rest A While

From the world of music we can learn the value of rest. The great volume of a musical theme is punctuated and embellished by 'rests' – a silent beat or two of the conductor, a pause between movements of a symphony.

In the monastic singing of the psalms there is an asterisk for a short pause, half way through the verse. Rest gives time for the theme or meaning to sink in – a breathing space.

Jesus is the master of movement and rest.

His apostles had gone out, full of enthusiasm, to preach. And with almost childlike excitement they came back to tell him 'all that they had done and taught.' (Mk.6:30) The hectic pace of work had taken control of them. 'Many were coming and going, and they had no leisure even to eat.' (Mk 6:30)

Jesus saw their need to steady down the tempo of their apostolate, to bring them to a place apart from the crowd. 'Come away by yourselves to a lonely place, and rest a while.' (Mk 6:31)

To all of us, wherever our lives or work are placed, Jesus gives us the same invitation. He sees our need to come apart – to relax, to think, to pray.

He took them and withdrew apart … (Lk 9:10)

Lord, give me the joy of coming apart into your presence,
and there to rest a while.

Revealed To Children

Jesus thanked his Father for revealing to little ones what he had hidden from the wise ones. What he revealed was the marvel of his love expressed in an invitation to 'Come to me, all you who labour and are heavy laden, and I will give you rest.' (Mt 11:28)

There came a moment when the world was heavy laden with the burden of a terrible war, when Mary came with a message and invitation through 'little ones', three young children of Fatima, Francisco, Jacinta, and Lucia,on 13 May 1917.

Her message was an appeal for prayer and penance, and a desire that the world would be consecrated to her Immaculate Heart. It was preceded by a preparation. An angel came and gave them a formula which became an unceasing refrain in their prayer: 'My God, I believe, I adore, I love.'

Mary drew them upward along a path to heroic holiness. Their words give an insight into the pure and simple form of their holiness. Francisco: 'I was thinking of Jesus who is so sad because of the sins that are committed against him.' Jacinta: 'How beautiful God is! But he is sad because of the sins of men. I want to suffer for love of him.'

When declaring them Blessed on 13 May 2000, Pope John Paul II said: 'Mary speaks to them with a mother's voice and heart; she asks them to offer themselves as victims of reparation, saying that she was ready to lead them safely to God. And behold, they see a light shining from her maternal hands which penetrates them inwardly, so that they feel immersed in God just as – they explain – a person sees himself in a mirror.'

I bless you Father … for hiding these things from the learned and clever, and revealing them to little children. (Mt.11:25)

Immaculate Mother, we pray you, through the intercession of Blessed Francisco and Blessed Jacinta, to help us to live the message of Fatima, and to find, through your Immaculate Heart, access to the Heart of your Son.

Sail On

At a time when St John of the Cross was beset by grave problems he used to read the account of the voyage of discovery of Columbus, and how at one stage of the voyage some of the crew were on the point of mutiny. They were frightened of the journey into the unknown. St John used to write each day in his log book just two words: 'Sail on.'

For all of us there can be a dark ocean which we have to cross and we cannot avoid fear of the hazard of the journey and of the peril of the unknown.

A sea journey in war time carries an added hazard. My memory is still vivid of such a voyage from Folkstone to Boulogne. Several hundred passengers were on board, all of us standing on deck, some wearing life jackets. At various points officers were watching the sea for a possible periscope of a submarine. Darkness was falling, and there were no harbour lights which in peace time could relieve the discomfort of a stormy crossing.

It is possible still to remember precisely the date, 23 October 1939. How impressive to read a year ago a poem composed by St Faustina, dated 20 October 1937:

> The barque of my life sails along amid the darkness
> and shadows of night, and I see no shore.
> The slightest storm would drown me,
> Engulfing my boat in the swirling waters.
> Amid the roaring waves I sail peacefully, trustingly,
> Because You, O Jesus, are my Light.

We need the faith of St John of the Cross and the confidence of St Faustina to help us to keep sailing on.

> ***And he awoke and rebuked the wind,***
> ***and said to the sea, 'Peace, be still.' (Mk 4:39)***

> *Lord, protect me in the storm.*
> *Bring all who are caught in a stormy sea safely to land.*

Saint Joseph

An Italian artist carved a statue of St Joseph in wood. He showed him holding in his hands the Basilica of St Peter.

Thus he brings visibly before us the mission of St Joseph as patron of the universal Church. It is fitting that he be guardian of the universal family, who had the care of the Child and his Mother.

His is a story without words, yet eloquent with many qualities. His life was a meeting-place of faith and love and obedience. He bowed in unquestioning faith before the mystery of the Incarnation. His obedience to various directives he received was instant.

His status was acknowledged by an angel. 'Rise, take the child and his mother.' (Mt 2:20) His position in the family was recognised by Mary: 'Your father and I have been looking for you anxiously.' (Lk 2:48)

St Bernardine of Siena helps our appreciation of St Joseph. 'Whenever divine grace selects someone to receive particular grace, all the gifts for his state are given to that person to enrich him abundantly … this is true of Joseph who was chosen to be the guardian of the most precious treasures of God, his Son and his spouse.'

'It is beyond doubt that Christ did not deny to Joseph in heaven that intimacy, respect, and high honour which he showed to him as to a father during his own human life.'

We can be sure of the power of his intercession, as was St Teresa of Avila who said: 'I do not remember even now that I ever asked anything of him which he has failed to grant.'

And he went down with them and came to Nazareth, and was obedient to them. (Lk 2:51)

Jesus, Mary and Joseph, I give you my heart and my soul. Be with me on my way.

Sight And Sound

Two composers found in the sea inspiration for distinguished musical compositions. Debussy was fascinated by vision – the sight of the sea with the even rhythmic movements of the waves, the sun dancing on the water. He composed 'La Mer'.

Vaughan Williams was captivated by hearing – the sound of the waves breaking against the cliffs, the sounding thunder rumbling up from the deep.

Sight and sound. To see and to hear. We might transfer the insights from the world of music to the world of faith. Our baptismal candle symbolises the visible light which plays on every day of our pilgrim journey, a vision that penetrates to a world beyond. Cardinal Newman describes it: 'The Christian penetrates through the veil of this world and sees the next.' We have the lovely words of St Clement: 'Through faith the eyes of our hearts are opened, and our dim clouded understanding unfolds like a flower to the light.'

Faith comes also by hearing. Mary was declared blessed because she believed. She was the one who above all heard the word of God and kept it. Mary Magdalene recognised the risen Lord by hearing his voice.

The celebration of the birth of the Lord is, as was his first coming, a mystery which was revealed by seeing and hearing. Each year it is a call to an intense and constant prayer for an increase in the grace of seeing and hearing.

The shepherds returned, glorifying and praising God
for all they had heard and seen. (Lk 2:19)

Lord, show me your face, and open my ears to hear your word.

Sign Of The Rainbow

In the Rosary Basilica in Lourdes there are fifteen chapels representing the mysteries of the rosary.

The artist who designed the mosaic in the chapel of the annunciation traced in the background a rainbow. In the moment of Mary's serene acceptance of the divine motherhood, and entrance of the Redeemer into the world, a rainbow, spanning the heavens, was a fitting symbol to describe his saving love.

Like Noah, mankind can for ever see the rainbow as the sign of God's covenant, proclaiming his never-ending love of his people. 'I set my bow in the cloud, and it shall be a sign of the covenant between me and the earth.' (Gen 9:13)

In the presence of that Annunciation mosaic we might like to read the words in the Book of Sirach: 'Look upon the rainbow and praise him who made it, exceedingly beautiful in its brightness. It encircles the heavens with its glorious arc, the hands of the most high have stretched it out.' (Sir 43:11, 12)

The rainbow can help us to enter into Mary's joy that the mercy of her Son would extend from east to west, his arms extended on the cross in a universal embrace.

A rainbow in the sky gives us joy. It tells us that the storm is over. The rainbow of salvation is the sign that the battle against sin is over and so we can, for ever, rejoice.

Far as the east is from the west,
so does he remove our transgressions from us. (Ps 103:12)

Lord, fold me in your loving embrace.

Signposts For Eternity

When travelling a new road we are helped by road signs. They give us information and keep us on course towards our destination.

On our Christian pilgrim journey the road is new to us. The saints are along our road, helping us both as light and example. They are for us signposts to eternity. Just as each, by his or her message and style of holiness, meets the needs of a particular time, so also are they for us in our personal lives.

'They fix the Church more firmly in holiness. By their fraternal concern is our weakness greatly helped.' (*The Church,* Vat II)

François Mauriac describes the power of their intercession: 'They prevent us, poor travellers on earth, from being frightened of the dark, they help us to march forward into the night without losing heart. I open my missal on Holy Saturday night where there is the Litany of the Saints… I call to you one by one by your names. I conjure up your innumerable army, silent but eternally alive, confessors, virgins, penitents, apostles, martyrs, jubilant procession of the Lamb.'

We have our own personal litany of the saints. It is worthwhile to keep them part of our daily prayer.

You are fellow citizens with the saints
and members of the household of God. (Eph 2:19)

Lord, increase my faith in the power of the intercession of the saints.

Spreading The Good News

'The Church on earth is by its nature missionary, since, according to the plan of the Father she has as her origin the mission of the Son and the Holy Spirit.' The *Catechism of the Catholic Church*, using the words of the Second Vatican council, explains the origin and purpose of the Church.

Jesus, both by practice and by preaching fulfilled his missionary purpose. He was ever moving forward. Having preached in one place he must soon be on his way to 'other cities'.

'The Holy Spirit leads the Church on her missionary path, and in the course of history, unfolds the mission of Christ. And from the Day of Pentecost the church has never lost its first fervour. Across the hills and valley of countries and continents, missionaries have been ever on the road.

G. K. Chesterton said that a feature of the history of the Church is that flowers are always springing up in the desert. The joy and consolation of missionaries must be the result of their work in a great flowering of Christian life, so often from tiny beginnings.

We are all meant to be part of the great missionary apostolate, linked with it through our constant prayer.

Pope Paul VI described the place of each of us in the missionary role of the Church: 'The Christian community is never closed in upon itself … it is the whole Church that receives the mission to evangelise, and the work of each individual member is important to the whole'.

Mary was the first missionary, rising up and going with haste across the hill country, bringing the Lord across a new threshold. When she journeyed across the hills it was high springtime, and her presence brings to the missionary apostolate the mood and freshness of springtime.

How beautiful upon the mountains are the feet of him who brings good tidings. (Is 52:7)

Mary, Queen of the Missions, pray for us.

Stay Near Me, Lord

Sometimes a thought, a simple pleading, can more easily be expressed in verse than in prose. Here is a prayer of the heart which I put together in verse form:

> Stay near me,Lord, until the daylight fades;
> And in the dark, give me your hand to clasp.
> And when the night is passed, and daylight comes,
> Give me your grace; light up another day.
>
> To troubled hearts, give shelter in the storm;
> To all in pain, bring comfort and relief;
> To all who hunger, be the Bread of Life;
> Sustain our hope, until we meet again.
>
> May all your people, sharing the one Bread,
> Be one in heart, grow daily in your love;
> May all who come to be refreshed in hope,
> Go forth in peace, to love and serve you, Lord.

Stay with us, for it is towards evening. (Lk 24:29)

Lord, I pray you, stay close by me every passing hour.

Sunset At Ballyconneely

From the strand at Ballyconneely near Clifden, I looked in wonderment at a summer sunset. In the minutes before sundown, the sun like a great golden ball of fire seemed to be sitting on the rim of the ocean.

Then, quickly and visibly the setting sun slipped below the rim of the water, and in a few minutes had disappeared from view.

My first reaction was a sense of loneliness, of loss. The day was done, and could not be retrieved. The French have a saying: 'Parting is a kind of death.' Watching the sunset was an experience of parting. How can you cope with parting without a tinge of sadness? How say goodbye to a millennium without any kind of nostalgia for our life's span which covers the latter part of the century?

To find the answer, there was but to turn and look eastwards, and there before one's eyes was a range of mountains, the Twelve Pins, their peaks standing out clearly against a crystal clear blue sky. Somehow they conveyed the sense of presence, of permanence, a kind of symbol of eternity.

They immediately brought to mind another thought that relieves the sense of loss at the sunset. As Jacob neared the end of his life he blessed his son Joseph. He looked forward to the moment when the promised Messiah would come, and he prayed 'the blessings of your father are strengthened with the blessings of his father until the desire of the everlasting hills should come.' (Gen 49:26)

Jesus, who is the desire of the everlasting hills, keeps the desire of the eternal day alive in our hearts.

Your sun shall no more go down ...
for the Lord will be your everlasting light. (Is 60:20)

Heart of Jesus, desire of the everlasting hills, have mercy on us.

The Good Shepherd

In the ancient church of Galla Placida at Ravenna, among the famous mosaics is one of the shepherd and sheep. It depicts the Good
Shepherd, seated on a hillock, and on the slope on either side are
ranged sheep, and they are all turned and looking towards the shepherd. The scene depicts the centrality of the shepherd and the unity
with and the care for him of the sheep.

In his preaching to the first Christians, St Peter used the image
of the sheep and the shepherd. 'You were straying like sheep, but
have now returned to the Shepherd and Guardian of your souls.' (1
Pet 2:24)

Here we have a graphic image of the Church – the flock are
'turned towards' the shepherd, not only with their eyes but with
their hearts.

The affection of the first Christians for Peter and Paul comes
through in various moments of their history. Their care for Peter:
'So Peter was kept in prison; but earnest prayer for him was made to
God by the church.' (Acts 12:5). The moment of departure of Paul:
'he knelt down and prayed with them all. And they all wept and
embraced Paul and kissed him.' (Acts 20:36)

The same ideal holds for the Church today. for the successor of
Peter: love for his person, assent to his teaching, prayer for his pastoral mission in the world of today.

I am the good shepherd; I know my own and my own know me.
(Jn 10:14)

Lord, deepen my love for the Church.

The Call

A leader in business or politics starts his term by choosing his council or cabinet. He knows them. He builds his programme around them.

At the start of his public mission Jesus chose his apostles. The initiative was his. He called them. He needed no time to decide on them. He already knew them, and 'immediately he called them'. (Mk 1:20)

Equally prompt was their reply. 'Immediately they left their nets and followed him.' (Mk 1:18) Theirs was a total and for all time giving themselves to him. A remarkable event. He called them just as they were, in their working clothes, Simon and Andrew casting a net, James and John mending their nets. They left everything behind – boat, their way of life; nets, the fruit of their work; their father, their home.

He took them into a personal companionship. He made them 'to be with him'. They became his cherished possession. He made them 'his own'. 'He called them to him those whom he desired, and they came to him.' (Mk 3:13)

Today, as in the gospel, Jesus calls. Here is the beginning of a vocation to the priesthood or religious life. His call is now and, as then, generous hearts respond. They come to him.

Bossuet has an impressive reflection on vocation: 'Come, Andrew and Simon. You are nobody. You have nothing. There is nothing in you which deserves to be sought. There is simply a vast capacity to be filled. Come to receive; come to be filled at the infinite source.'

Jesus, having loved his own who were in the world,
he loved them to the end. (Jn 13:1)

Lord Jesus, strengthen and encourage those who are called
to the priesthood and religious life.

The Carpenter's Son

In human relationships, one way of trying to lower a person's status is to trace him back to his humble beginnings – as the phrase goes, to cut him down to size.

Jesus was subjected to that kind of behaviour. Sharp and bitter tongues voiced the question: 'Is not this the carpenter's son? Is not his mother called Mary?' (Mt 13:55) And it is all the more poignant, occuring 'in his own country'.

Down through the centuries that cry has gone up. Christ is nothing more than the carpenter. They cannot recognise him when he was cut down to size on the wood of the cross. Nor do they see Mary as more than just the carpenter's wife.

Who is this Jesus Christ? Lacordaire gives the answer in a sublime word picture:

'This man has been attached to a cross for centuries, but each day thousands of people take him down from his throne of suffering; they kneel before him, they prostrate themselves as low as they can before him, they kiss his bleeding feet with inexpressible ardour. This man was scourged, crucified, and killed; but an unspeakable love resurrected him from death and from infamy.

This man is the only human being ever to have founded a kingdom of love on earth; and this man is you, O Jesus Christ!'

Truly this was the Son of God. (Mt 27:54)

My Lord and my God.

The Cherry Tree

Father Congar OP tells of a cherry tree in the garden of his home. One day it was struck by lightening. It was almost totally destroyed except for one branch left hanging by a thread. That one branch continued to produce cherries.

He kept on working in spite of his failing health. He was able to read into the history of that cherry tree a message: the will to keep on going and doing what he could. The Holy Spirit would give him the will to keep going, and to be content with whatever little he could do.

It's a story with a valuable message for us, applied to many life experiences in different settings. It can happen in the area of opportunity or ability to work, limitations caused by illness or age, tensions in the effort to hold on to harmony or unity in marriage, successive disappointments of youth in career achievement, when all that seems to be left is to hold on by a string.

Such is the moment to pray for strength to avoid despondency, to keep clear of the feeling that life has fallen apart and that there is nothing left. The slender branch of the tree kept producing cherries, even though holding on just by a thread. The Lord turns our weakness into strength. The particular qualities we need, whether courage or patience or hope, he does not fail to give us.

By this my Father is glorified, that you bear much fruit,
and so prove to be my disciples. (Mt 15:8)

Lord, I ask you for the courage to keep going,
and to use fruitfully the time and space you give me.
Help all who are hanging on by a thread to life or hope.

The Contemplatives

The purpose and value of the contemplative life has been well summarised by Cardinal Newman: 'The occasional retreat of the many requires the lifelong retreat of the few. To be shut off from the world is their very duty to the world. To be in leisure is their business.'

The phrase 'flight from the world' is often used to describe their journey into the desert, but it can also be understood as a flight *for* the world. Their location is a place of desert stillness where listening, which is their first activity, is possible. Their active attention to the voice of God leads on to seeking, in a never-ending adventure of a new finding him.

That vocation requires leisure which means space for 'the work of God', an unending prayer of praising and pleading.

The family of Religious pleads for the human family – for all who are struggling to live, longing for peace in the restless, fretful pell mell of life. Like Moses, on the mountain, with hands outstretched during battle, the contemplatives keep hands lifted in prayer for all those, down in the lowlands, who are struggling to survive against the ways and the drag of the world.

As well, they have kept alive the essential values of permanence, order, peace, when, time and again, the whole fabric of life in the world around had fallen apart.

St Thomas Aquinas summarises their contribution to the world – 'to hand on the fruit of their contemplation to others'.

Their witness enriches all of us, reminding us that our Christian life needs a contemplative dimension, so that God is at the centre. We need listening with attention, a vision in sharp focus, our hearts directed towards the ultimate, finding him in eternal life.

Be still and know that I am God. (Ps 46:10)

Lord, build round my heart a zone of silence so that I may hear your voice. May I praise and thank you each day, and may my prayer help those who are trying to find you in their lives.

The Cushion

What a simple but valuable possession is a cushion! At the end of a day's work the ease of a cushioned chair soothes fatigue at evening time. And when we settle down to sleep a cushion as pillow beneath our head helps us towards that relaxation and peace that is the anti-room to slumber. How often, when the body aches in a bed of pain can a cushion placed in support of the aching part bring some relief.

A cushion has been given honorable mention in the gospel. At the end of a day's work Jesus was tired.He wished to draw back from the crowd 'Let us go across to the other side.' (Mk 4:35) 'And leaving the crowd, the disciples took him, just as he was in the boat ... he was in the stern, asleep on the cushion.' (Mk 4:36-38)

What a touching picture! Jesus, perfectly human, subject to fatigue. For all time, he who felt tired at the end of the day, is aware of our fatigue, and rewards us with sleep. What a comfort was that cushion that provided rest for the Saviour of the world, as he laid his head upon it!

A hymn of Good Friday addresses the wood of the Cross, asking the beams to bend a little, and so become pliable, as a form of cushion, to give some relief to the dying Jesus.

I will lie down in peace, and sleep comes at once. (Ps 4:8)

Lord, I pray you to give me the soothing gift of sleep,
and cushion the suffering of all those who are in pain this night.

The Diamond Rocks

At Kilkee, Co Clare, at the base of enormous cliffs, there is a massive reef of rocks, jutting out into the sea, They are called the Diamond Rocks.

Every few minutes, a huge incoming wave of swirling water rushes in over them, and as it quickly recedes it leaves a great coating of beautiful white spray, like a great washing powder that covers the rocks, and then slips back into the sea, leaving them like a sparkling diamond.

And the same motion keeps repeating every few minutes, as another great mountain of water gathers momentum, till it also spreads over the rocks. Watching the power and beauty and purity of that movement of the sea, one felt that it contained a message.

I recalled the reflection of the Curé of Ars: 'God's mercy is like an unleashed torrent, it bears away all hearts in its flow.'

The great surging wave, cleansing and polishing the diamond rocks, brings easily to mind the great ocean of mercy that flows from the heart of Jesus in the sacrament of Penance. And like the continuous incoming ocean waves, there comes from his Heart a fountain, never ending, of sacramental life.

To watch the repeated cleansing of a reef of rocks can carry us forward in our conviction of the value of our repeated use of this sacrament.

And as the rocks are already clean before the wave arrives, so our souls, even when already clean, are still further enriched because we have thus acknowledged our awareness and thanks for the grace of the divine mercy of the Lord.

Wash me, and I shall be whiter than snow. (Ps 50:7)

Lord, have mercy on me, and cleanse me from my sins.

The Divine Motherhood

When the Fathers of the Council of Ephesus, led by St Cyril of Alexandria, were coming from the Council after the definition of the divine motherhood, they were greeted by the people with a torchlight procession. Thus was symbolised the joy of the universal Church, saluting Mary, Mother of God.

The marvel of Mary's motherhood is described by Abbot Vonier OSB. Her divine motherhood is 'a masterpiece of God's wisdom. It is a source of spiritual power, the foundation of an immense hope … The whole of creation stands in awe before the overpowering glory of that blessed vision – the Mother with her child.'

What was defined at Ephesus was further illumined by the Second Vatican Council. Placing its reflection on Mary within the *Dogmatic Constitution on the Church,* it presents Mary as model of the Church, exemplar both of virginity and motherhood.

'In a certain way she unites and mirrors within herself the central truths of the faith. Hence when she is being preached and venerated, she summons the faithful to her Son and his sacrifice, and to love of the Father.'

She 'summons': it is the summons of love by a mother. She gives our lives a threefold direction – to her Son, to his sacrifice, and to love of the Father.

They saw the child with Mary his mother. (Mt 2:11)

Mary, Mother of God and Mother of the Church, pray for us.

The Drama Of Lovers

Calvary was called by St Francis de Sales 'The drama of lovers'.

While a chorus of mockery and derision rose up from the crowd around Calvary, the voices of three lovers around the cross were silent. But love has its own language, and the unspoken language of love from Mary, John and Magdalene, must have comforted the dying Jesus.

The prophet had said: 'They shall look…', and what eyes but theirs must have feasted on the glorious vision of his heart in that solemn hour?

It was fitting that they should be present.

Mary, with the instinct of motherhood, could not be absent. It was her finest hour. In majestic silence she stood, giving him her mother love in its most sublime expression. Two hearts became one: his, opened on the altar of his body, hers pierced on the altar of her heart.

John had leaned close to the Master's breast at the supper. Now, again, close to his heart, he enriched us for all time by recording those whispered secrets of Jesus on the cross. Here was the moment and the place of origin of what future generations would call devotion to the Heart of Jesus.

Magdalene gave the tribute of tears. The magnetism of his love had drawn her. She could not bear to be away from him or without him, and so she was at the foot of the Cross, as in the garden of Easter she would be frantically seeking and finding him, and falling at his feet.

There they crucified him. (Jn 19:18)

We adore you, O Christ, and praise you,
because by your holy Cross you have redeemed the world.

The Enigma Of Suffering

Paul Claudel throws a light that helps us to understand the enigma of suffering: 'Jesus came not to suppress suffering, nor to explain it, but to fill it with his presence.'

St Paul, the great lover, shows how, through suffering, his heart was filled with the presence of his crucifed Lord: 'I have been crucified with Christ; it is no longer I who live, but Christ lives in me.' (Gal 2:20) His was a remarkable story of loss and again. 'For his sake I have suffered the loss of all things, and count them as refuse, in order that I might gain Christ.' (Phil 3:8)

Near to our time we might select, from so many lovers of the cross, two whose witness can inspire us.

St Bernadette of Lourdes: With heroic courage she endured suffering at an extreme level. 'I am ground like a grain of wheat.' Her example was to teach us the redemptive value of suffering. 'O most compassionate heart of my Jesus, accept each of my tears, each cry of pain from me as a supplication for all those who suffer, for all those who weep, for all those who forget you.'

St Thérèse of the Child Jesus similarly bore suffering during her whole life, not only with outstanding patience, but with joy. Her witness was to be fashioned in love through pain. Her poetic words describe the journey through the dark night into the light of spring: 'The snowdrop endures the testing time of winter before it comes up through the snow into the warm sunshine of spring.'

We are all learners in the school of suffering. Well for us that we have such expert teachers.

If any man would come after me, let him deny himself, take up his cross and follow me. (Mt 16:24)

Lord, give me the courage to bear and offer my sufferings for love of you. Give comfort and relief to the sick.

The Fifth Evangelist

Some time ago when restoration of a medieval church on the pilgrim road from Rome to Monte Cassino was completed, a fresco was discovered on the wall of the façade. It showed five figures, four of which were identified as the evangelists, and the fifth was taken as representing the prophet Isaiah. That title has often been given to him, because his prophecy is so vivid and detailed that it seems as if he had been a witness of the whole drama of salvation.

It is worth our while to make him our constant companion, and as we turn over the pages we may find each time some insight, within a short phrase which seems to come to life for us, that we had not discovered before.

'Come let us climb the mountain of the Lord, and he will show us his ways.' (Is 2:3) We might accept his invitation to travel and live the central events of the mystery, as told by him. His words are like a great spotlight that plays on those events:

'The people that walked in darkness have seen a great light.' (Is 9:2)

'For to us a child is born.' (Is 9:6)

'He will feed his flock like a shepherd.' (Is 40:11)

'Comfort, comfort, my people.' (Is 40:1)

'He was despised and rejected by men.' (Is 53:3)

'Arise, shine, for your light has come.' (Is 60:1)

Isaiah conveys to us a message of consolation, a motive for gratitude, a reason for joy.

With everlasting love I will have compassion on you. (Is 54:8)

Lord Jesus, teach me your ways.
May we all find happiness in following your steps.

The Final Triumph

The closing act or chapter of a great drama generally brings the threads together with a happy ending.

The Ascension brought to a triumphant conclusion the drama of Jesus. Blessed Columba Marmion OSB describes it: 'In a sense, the Ascension is the greatest feast, because it is the supreme glorification of Christ Jesus. Holy Church calls this Ascension 'admirable' and 'glorious'.' It opened the prospect of eternal life through his passion, death and resurrection.

For all time it is a foretaste of the life to come. It invites us, as the apostles, to direct our hearts above. In the words of St Leo, 'In the person of Christ we have penetrated the heights of heaven.'

But, in the meantime, life has to be lived. 'While they were gazing into heaven as he went, behold two men stood by them in white robes, and said, "Men of Galilee, why do you stand looking into heaven?" ' Vision would end, but his presence would remain through the coming of the Holy Spirit.

'Hope related to the end of time does not diminish the importance of intervening duties.' (*The Church Today*, Vat II)

While he blessed them, he departed from them. And they worshipped him, and returned to Jerusalem with great joy.
(Lk 24:51, 52)

Lord, through the grace of your Ascension,
keep my heart focused on eternal life.

The Four Freedoms

An International Eucharistic Congress was held in Wroclaw, Poland in preparation for the millennium. The theme of the Congress was 'Eucharist and freedom'.

In his Eucharistic hymn, *'Verbum Supernum'*, St Thomas Aquinas admirably describes the gift of freedom which we receive through the Eucharist, under four headings. We might use the title of a plan to restore a world devastated by war, 'The four freedoms', for freedom related to the Eucharist:

By being born he gave us companionship,

At the Supper he gave us food,

On the Cross he was our ransom,

Reigning in glory, he gives us reward.

By being born he became Emmanuel, God with us. In the Eucharist he gave us a companionship that will never end. Never again need we be lonely. In our most desolate hours his eucharistic presence consoles us,

At the Supper he gave us food. For all time, freedom from hunger. At the Last Supper, his invitation was offered to all and for ever, 'Take, all of you and eat.'

On the Cross he freed us from sin. From his wounded side flows a fountain of sacramental life.

Reigning in glory, he gives reward, freedom to hope. The Eucharist is the pledge of future glory. He puts into our hearts a forward impulse – waiting to greet him when he comes again.

He who eats this bread will live for ever. (Jn 6:58)

Lord, make my heart free to love you more and more.

The Homecoming Of God

There is a poem of G. K. Chesterton called 'The Neglect of Christmas':

There fared a maiden driven forth,
Out in the hills to roam
In the place where she was homeless,
All men are at home.

It tells a story that will never lose its freshness, its pathos. And as long as there are hearts open to the beauty of childhood and to the appeal of a God who is young and helpless and full of mercy, it will continue to move hearts as it moved St Francis of Assisi to tears.

A maiden driven forth: a sinful world tucking itself away for sleep closes the doors on God coming to take its sins away. A strange welcome, to find himself homeless among his own.

And yet, year by year, or more often if we are wise, we go over to Bethlehem and in that hillside cave we find ourselves at home.

There the divine drama begins. Shepherds adore the Good Shepherd as he comes. The song of angels that greets his coming will fuse with the Alleluias that will herald his coming forth from the tomb. It is one song, the sweetest music ever heard on earth, that the Prince of Peace, born for us, dying for us, will win the day for us, and thus earn for us a home. Let us rejoice!

The word became flesh and dwelt among us. (Jn 1:14)

Come, let us adore Christ the Lord.

The Invisible Link

In an Irish novel of Canon Sheehan is described a moment of the parting of two friends. 'They parted without grief, knowing that an invisible link in the heart of Jesus held them together.'

In different settings we find the same idea.

St Thérèse of Lisieux tells of the moment shortly after she entered Carmel. Her father became gravely ill. Having lost her mother when she was very young, she had a very tender affection for her father. Once she entered Carmel it was no longer possible for her to be with him. On learning of his illness she wrote to him: 'Even though oceans divide us, our hearts are together.' For hearts so united, no distance could sever the link that bound them together. Her awareness of that invisible link made it possible for her to accept the distance that divided them, and she wrote in the same letter: 'I opened my arms to suffering and embraced it with great love.'

St Teresa Benedicta Stein, having received the faith in adult life, developed a very tender love of the Heart of Jesus. After she became a Carmelite nun she was, at one moment, being transferred from Beuron to another convent, and she wrote to a friend, Mother Petra: 'Physical separation cannot keep us apart if we are united with God.'

The awareness of the invisible link can be deep in meaning. It is a vivid description of what might be called a spirituality of parting. A consoling thought – whether in the parting of friends, for a while or for longer, or in the parting in death – we do not lose them. In the Heart of Jesus we remain and find one another.

Beloved, let us love one another. (1 Jn 4:7)

Lord, keep my friends in your loving care.

The Journey

A poet can clothe profound ideas in attractive words. Here is a lovely poem by the American poet, Robert Frost:

The woods are lovely, dark and deep,

But I have promises to keep,

and miles to go before I sleep.

We might think of it as describing the journey of life in three acts.

And as we follow the course of the drama we might link it with the words of the Prophet Baruch: 'The woods and every fragrant tree have shaded Israel at God's command. For God will lead Israel with joy in the light of his glory.' (Bar.5:8)

Life's adventure through unseen paths, along narrow ways, is like a forest journey. The experience of the forest with its stillness can be 'lovely' in those days when life goes smoothly; it can be 'deep' at that moment in the forest when the 'long' path leads us into deep and dangerous tracks, when we are fearful of losing our way, when the darkness of unexpected trials or pain become part of our daily journey.

Lord, as I settle down in your presence to pray, surround my heart with the lovely stillness of the forest. As you shaded Israel, let me rest beneath your shadow as a forest traveller takes repose beneath a fragrant tree.

I have made promises to keep: to be faithful, to be loving, to be trusting. Promises made with joy, but through the wear and tear of life they can come under strain. Keep them fresh in my memory.

As the road opens out before me day by day, I ask you, Lord, to stay close by me at every step. As you led Israel with joy, lead me to the light of your glory. Before I sleep I have no fear of the close, just sleeping a while before waking up to eternal life.

Make me know your ways, O Lord. (Ps 25:4)

Lord, give me strength to complete my journey.

The Landscape Painter

A landscape painter was asked on a TV programme what was her approach to painting. She replied, 'I never paint a road that doesn't open out on to something. I never paint regret.'

A talented artist with a noble ideal. She never paints a cul-de-sac. Her mind, like her brush, moves forward, not like a traveller, looking back sadly along the road of yesterday, clinging to memories of a past that has gone.

She conveys a message that we can apply to moments on our journey when we can only see ahead of us, a cul-de-sac. Those blighted hopes and failed projects tend to form a kind of road block, when we can see no road opening before us. Burdened with dreams of lost horizons and vain regrets, we can't move forward.

Is there not, in a story of Easter Day, something illustrated in the approach of that landscape painter? Two men on the road from Jerusalem, travelling with their shattered dreams. Their Lord on the Cross, and the prospect of a restored kingdom gone. They were travelling a closed road, overcome with regret. 'We had hoped.' (Lk 24:21) They were a perfect picture of regret. 'They stood still, looking sad.' (Lk 24:17)

Then the divine Stranger joined them, opening up to them a vista, showing them a road, not just to Emmaus but a road on and on into eternity. 'He seemed to be going further.' (Lk 24:28)

The millennium brings us an invitation to take the road on a great adventure of faith, on a road that is ever opening out before us. On that road there is no place for regret. It is the road of hope.

Lord, teach me your paths. (Ps 25:4)

Lord, strengthen my hope on my road to you.
Make life for all of us a road of hope, always opening out before us.

The Language Of Prayer

An old and poor woman, living in a little room on the top flat of a tenement, when I asked her, 'Who is here with you?' replied 'Nobody but God and myself.' She lived in poverty, but was rich in faith.

It has been said that the poor have taught us the language of prayer. Right throughout the sacred story, poverty is a condition that evokes the beginning of prayer, a pleading that reaches the ears of God, and always finds a response. 'This poor man cried, and the Lord heard him and saved him from all his troubles.' (Ps 34:6) 'I am poor and needy, but the Lord has taken thought of me.' (Ps 40:17)

Jesus, coming into this world, 'being rich, became poor for our sakes.' (2 Jas 8:9) When announcing a new way of life and happiness, he placed poverty as the first of the beatitudes. 'Blessed are the poor in spirit for theirs is the kingdom of heaven.' (Mt 5:3)

The spirit of poverty creates a sense of dependence on the merciful God. The person who has nothing is an empty vessel, 'God's beggars,' St Augustine calls all of us, whose humble prayer God answers.

In a world where the culture of success tends to take over, and the illusion of power which material wealth creates, there is need to relearn the first beatitude, that true riches are the reward for poverty of spirit.

It is good for us, in the context of that beatitude, to reflect on the words of St James: 'Has not God chosen the poor of this world to be rich in faith and heirs of the kingdom which God has promised to those who love him?' (Jas 2:5)

Incline your ear, O Lord. Answer me, for I am poor and afflicted.
(Ps 86:l)

Lord Jesus, listen to my prayer, for I am poor and need your help.

The Light Of Day

At the beginning of his public life Jesus announced that he had been sent to open the eyes of the blind. His last miracle on his way from Jericho to Jerusalem was to give sight to a poor blind man on the road.

A simple cry from the heart, 'Jesus, Son of David, have mercy on me', (Lk 18:35) touched his heart. Just one simple request was enough: 'Lord, let me receive my sight.' Jesus touched his eyes. 'Your faith has made you well', and immediately he received his sight and followed him on the way. (18:35-43)

What an experience! What reward for his faith! To open his eyes for the first time to look straight into the eyes of the Redeemer. He was told that he could go his way, but his way became the way of Jesus.

Here is a lesson for us. We are all, in a sense, that blind man on the road. So often, these days, there are fears, crises – our road gets clouded in a fog of disbelief, a journey in the dark night.

We can learn from the gospel story a prayer from the heart: 'Lord, that I may see.' It is a prayer which, in the words of St John Climacus, 'knocks at the gates of heaven'.

The spirit of the Lord is upon me to proclaim
… recovering of sight to the blind. (Lk 4:18)

Lord, increase my faith so that I may see your way.
Give the comfort of your presence to the blind.

The Lights Of Home

In a poem of Francis Thompson we find these lines:
　　Tell them you grieve for your hearts know today;
　　Tell them you smile for your eyes see tomorrow.

A glance towards tomorrow helps to ease today's burden. We grieve today, but in the darkest hour of our sorrow the light of the glory that awaits us is already breaking. It is only when we forget the tomorrow of unending joy that the suffering of the present moment could become unbearable.

Our vision may be clouded by a mist of tears, but the lights of home are ever before us and, even though seen on a far horizon, they give us cheer.

Before he left this world Jesus gave us the key to the mystery of suffering. Sorrow now, but united with his, it refines our love and clears our vision. As he was starting on the way of the cross he invited us to share his burden, but in that very moment he was promising the joy that awaits us in his Father's home.

The way of the Cross is not a cul-de-sac. The road goes farther on, through Emmaus, through Galilee of his risen days, to the sunlit uphills, when we shall have eternal possession.

The thought of the glory to come is meant to colour and shape our lives, giving us the mentality and spirituality of pilgrims. The lights of home are coming near. Our eyes see tomorrow.

I consider that the sufferings of the present time are not worth comparing with the glory that is to be revealed to us. (Rom 8:18)

Lord, give me the grace to realise
that even when I walk in shadow I am in sunlight.
Give a bright tomorrow to those who grieve today.

The Lost Child

A chapter in a book by Caryll Houselander has the title, *The Lost Child*. She writes: 'There is nothing like the emptiness of a house from which a child has gone.' It describes the terrible vacuum in the parents' hearts, which no other person can fill.

Such was the grief of Mary and Joseph at the loss of the child, Jesus. We can imagine their anguish as they hurriedly searched Jerusalem for him, looking for him in every face. Theirs the distress of the spouse in the Canticle: 'Have you seen him whom my soul loves?' (Song 3:3)

And then the relief at finding him. His mother said: 'Son, why have you treated us so? Behold your father and I have been looking for you anxiously.' (Lk 2:4) It was one time when Mary spoke of her sorrow.

It would not be far-fetched for us to read a parallel between Mary's experience of abandonment during the three days' loss of her Son, and his three hours abandonment on the Cross. Two hearts united in pain.

Well for us that her mother love is ever active, searching for us when we sin.

I found him whom my soul loves. (Song 3:4)

Mary, my Mother, pray for the wanderer, pray for me.
Help parents in their search for a lost child.

The Magnetism Of Love

A magnet draws, and the object drawn responds to its impulse.

'I ... will draw all men to myself.' (Jn 12:32) It is never the way of Jesus to compel. When people refused to accept him, and walked no more with him, he let them go. When a city would not receive him, he passed on to another town.

And yet, many followed him and, down through the ages, a multitude, ever increasing in numbers, has been drawn to follow him and stay with him until the end. Why? Because the magnetism of his love has drawn them. In hearts that are open to him there arises an irresistible urge to come close to him.

A pagan poet once said: 'We are drawn by what pleases us.' St Augustine describes the source of the mysterious magnetism which Jesus exercises: 'We are drawn by love. No one who is unwilling is drawn.'

On the Cross, Jesus gave the supreme proof of his love, and from there he exercises a magnetism to draw countless human hearts to himself. 'I will draw all men to myself.' There is no resisting the beauty and urgency of that solemn promise. And we, in turn, like the lover in the Canticle, would long for his embrace: 'I held him and would not let him go.' (Song 3:4)

The promise of Jesus extends not just to a few privileged souls. He would draw 'all'. No one for whom he died is outside his universal embrace.

He has the power to lift. He has the love to draw. Only for us to pray, 'Lord, draw us.'

I am my beloved's and my beloved is mine. (Song 6:3)

Lord Jesus, draw me close to you,
so that I may always rejoice in your love.

The Missing Mail Bags

Long after a war ended, a quantity of mail bags containing post for soldiers at the front was found in a warehouse. With the best of intentions, through the hazards of war, the letters never reached their destination.

Sometimes we tend to wonder whether our requests in prayer, like the undelivered mail, reached their destination, the ear of God. But we can be sure that, while human ways can fail, our pleadings reach him, and receive his personal attention. They are not lost in transit.

Here are two sources that can reassure us:

The Book of Sirach gives us this consoling message – the direct line of our prayers from lips to ears: 'The prayer of a poor man goes from his lips to the ear of God.' (Sir 21:5)

St Augustine describes the upward ascent of our prayer: 'When prayer is sincerely uttered by a faithful heart, it rises as incense from a sacred altar.'

I waited, I waited for the Lord,
and he stooped down to me, he heard my cry. (Ps 39:1)

Lord, I thank you for always listening to my prayer.

The Moment Of Parting

'Oh that those lips had language,' begins a poem by William Cowper, composed on receiving a portrait of his mother.

Silent lips set off the beginning of grief. The companionship of language is broken. Yet, even though lips are silent, the unspoken language of love survives.

The living, consoling words of sacred scripture ease the most poignant sorrow. Often at a funeral Requiem Mass, a passage from the Apocalypse is chosen. Like the opening of a window letting in the sunlight, comes a message of a new heaven and a new earth, tears and mourning recede into the past tense. The Lord who is there from the beginning is there to open a new world.

The gospel tells of Jesus responding to a call of friends to be with them. From his heart there comes the gift of tears. His divine power promises the gift of life.

Cardinal Ratzinger recalls, in this context, Psalm 30, used in the liturgy of Holy Week. 'Weeping may tarry for the night, but joy comes with the morning.' He quotes St Paul: 'I consider that the sufferings of this present time are not worth comparing with the glory that is to be revealed to us.' (Rom 8:18)

'The centre of gravity of existence has shifted as a result of this certainty; now it lies at the morning of life, which means that it takes away the oppressiveness and the pressure of the moment, and dissolves the tears of evening by the power of a grace which lasts for ever. This is precisely what Easter faith is designed to give: the ability to look across from the evening to the morning, from the part to the whole, and thus to journey toward the joy of the redeemed which springs from that morning of the third day which first heard the message: Christ is risen!'

I am the resurrection and the life. (Jn 11:25)

Lord Jesus, grant me when I grieve,
the consolation of your presence and the joy of your resurrection.

The Mystery Of The Missing Parcel

There is a chapel in the Basilica of St Mary Major's in Rome where people gather daily for eucharistic adoration as well as to venerate an ancient icon of the Madonna, 'Salvation of the Roman people'.

One day a lady saw a small parcel on the floor beneath the seat where she was kneeling. In the world of that time there were frequent warnings of bomb scares and the danger of unattended packages. The lady drew the attention of others to this parcel, and instinctively everyone withdrew from the chapel, watching it silently from outside. At one stage the sacristan approached it, but he also withdrew.

Then an old little Italian woman pushed her way through the onlookers at the gate of the chapel, went in, took up the parcel, which was hers, and went her way.

In that little drama, perhaps, there is a message - that good and evil in our world often travel side by side. Truth and falsehood can co-exist in the spoken or written word. Packages, neatly wrapped, containing an assortment of half truths, can be planted in unexpected places, and be a potential hazard.

But, also, the story carries a reminder that we need not be too quickly frightened by dangers which, sometimes, we judge real but are only imaginary.

I fear no evil for thou art with me. (Ps 23:41)

Lord, from all the perils of the road,
whether great or small, keep me safe.

The Passion Play

At regular intervals the people of the town of Oberammergau present a passion play as an act of thanksgiving for their deliverance from a grave peril in the past.

The various parts in the drama are played by people of the town. One year the part of the 'Christus' was played by Anton Preisinger. After a performance he was found in a room alone, in tears and trembling all over. Playing the part of Christ he was overcome by the whole drama of the passion. He felt he was no longer playing a part, but was living the part. He was identifying with Christ in all the agony of his passion.

The reaction of this central actor in a passion play makes it easier for us to realise how deeply St Paul became one with Christ in his passion, so that he could say: 'I have been crucified with Christ; it is no longer I who live, but Christ who lives in me.' (Gal 2:20)

The passion play is a visual aid that brings clearly before us the drama of the Cross, to inspire us to unite ever more deeply to the sufferings of the crucified Jesus, and thus console him with a response of love.

If any man would come after me, let him deny himself,
take up his cross and follow me. (Mt 16:24)

Hail, O Cross, our only hope.

The Peace Of Bethany

Life can move with calm, but not always. Sometimes, within the space of just a few hours of any one day, can come in quick succession several darts of pain. How do I cope?

As always, Jesus is both my guide and teacher. Enough for me to turn my gaze on him in just one gospel moment when he experienced several painful trials.

He found the temple used for buying and selling, become a den of robbers. Then the painful sting of venomous tongues of chief priests: 'They were indignant.' (Mt 21:15)

What to do? He left them and went to Bethany. There he found the warmth of welcome of the loving hearts of Martha and Mary and Lazarus. Bethany and the love of true friends was a haven of peace. What a relief.

St Jerome describes the contrast: 'The Lord was so poor that he found no one in the big city who would offer him hospitality; no one gave him lodging. But in the company of Lazarus and his sisters he found welcome.'

Lord, there is another Bethany where I would wish to greet you, a Bethany in my heart to give you hospitality. Give me the generosity of heart of your Bethany friends to welcome you when you come to me in the person of someone who has been hurt in the wear and tear of life.

And leaving them, he went out of the city. (Mt 21:17)

Lord, at Bethany you stayed. Stay also with me.

The Prayer Of Asking

Often we feel that our efforts at prayer are more centred on asking than on thanking. I only seem to pray when I am asking for something.

At such a time it is useful for us to read again the words of Jesus: 'Ask, and it will be given you; seek, and you will find; knock, and it will be opened to you.' (Mt 7:7)

When we take him at his word we earn a double reward. He answers in the way that is best for us. And, as well, our very asking is a journey to him through the avenues of faith, hope and charity, and brings about a strengthening of those virtues which are the basis of our whole relationship with God.

That is how St Augustine interprets the threefold invitation of Jesus: We *ask* through *faith*. Because we believe in him we turn to him to ask his help. We *seek* through *hope*. Believing in his power we then set out on our journey of hope to seek him. We *knock* through *charity*. We knock at the door of the heart of him who is rich to all who call on him.

We can approach him with childlike confidence, knowing that he is ever ready to enrich us with his love – the love that reaches out to us by way of consolation, rescue, encouragement. He is attentive to our needs even before we ask. 'Before they call I will answer them.' (Is 65:24) He has a heart for each of us and at all times.

Reflecting on the prayer of asking and the prayer of thanks, Blessed Padre Pio recommended that when we ask Jesus for favours, we make sure to ask for the gift of his love, and then we shall readily move to the prayer of thanks to him for expanding our hearts to love him more.

Every one who asks receives, and he who seeks finds;
and to him who knocks it will be opened. (Lk 11:10)

Lord, with all my heart I ask your help.

The Prayer Of Childhood

Hilaire Belloc wrote a poem addressed to a child at evening prayer. 'And when at evening prayer completes the day,' he asked the child 'to pray for men who lose their fairylands'.

The fairyland of childhood is where is found the real world – of wonderment, joy, truth, innocence, dependence.

It is through the avenue of childhood that God revealed his love, and also the road to his heart. 'Israel was a child and I loved him … I taught Ephraim to walk. I took them in my arms.' (Hos 11:1, 3)

In Jesus the full reality of that tender image became visible. 'Calling to him a child he put him in the midst of them.' (Mt 18:2) He told his disciples that they must turn and become like children if they would enter the kingdom of heaven.

Not the apostles only, but all of us need to be taught. And, as a start, we can learn the prayer language of childhood. It is always simple and direct, a confident plea to the heavenly Father. 'Bend down your ear to hear me, and speedily rescue me.' (Ps 30:4) It is enough for us to whisper in his ear some secret request. We know he will listen. He never refuses.

'Let the children come to me.' (Lk 18:16) To all of us goes out the same invitation: enough that we have the candour of childhood.

Whoever humbles himself like this child,
he is the greatest in the kingdom of heaven. (Mt 18:4)

Lord, teach me to pray with the faith and love of a child.

The Prayer Of Twilight

There is a delightful scene described in the *Confessions* of St Augustine. He and his mother Monica are seated at evening time at a window of their home at Ostia. 'There we were alone in our joy thinking of the Truth.' Just the two of them, perfectly happy to be together, not even words necessary to express their joy.

The scene might be thought of as illustrating what is often called 'The prayer of twilight.'

Two friends seated at a fire, happy in each other's company. Unnoticed, the light fades towards dark till they are scarcely visible to each other. At a stage their conversation slows down till they are in silence. Yet in that twilight hour they are happy, just to be present to each other.

In the scene is there not something of a parallel with a moment when, in the quiet of evening we come into the sacramental presence of Jesus? In the twilight we are alone in our joy in his presence. At one stage we find that we don't need words. It is enough for us to be in his company. As St Augustine and St Monica were pondering the Truth, we ponder the marvel of the truth of his unending presence.

It is enough for us to look, to ponder, and to give ourselves time to be looked on by him.

In your presence there is fullness of joy. (Ps 16:11)

Lord, in your love draw me often into your presence.

The Question

'Whom do you seek?' (Jn 1:38) Three times in the gospel that question was posed by Jesus. They recall three special moments of revelation, of the divine drama of salvation – the call, the combat, the victory.

Can we relive those moments in his presence, listening to his voice, gentle and appealing, echoing from the depths of his heart?

The call: For Andrew and his companion, walking along the bank of the Jordan, the shadow of Jesus crossed their path for the first time. 'Jesus turned and saw them following him, and said to them "Whom do you seek?" And they said to him, "Rabbi (which means teacher) Where are you staying?" ' (Jn 1:39) And they received an invitation which changed their lives: 'Come and see.' They stayed with him that day. We cannot pierce the curtain of that evening encounter. What we do know is that in those few hours they became his.

The combat: In the darkness of the night of betrayal, Jesus for the second time asked 'whom do you seek?' His question was addressed, not to those who approached him in order to love him but to a crowd with evil in their hearts. A band of soldiers came to seize him.

The victory: Magdalene on Easter Day, 'turned and saw Jesus standing, and he said to her "Woman, why are you weeping? Whom do you seek?" ' (Jn 20:14) In her joy she worshipped him.

We also, through our seeking, find him. Pascal reminds us: 'We would not go on seeking him if we had not found him.'

Seek, and you will find. (Lk 11:9)

Lord, make me realise that every day you turn towards me
and ask 'whom do you seek? and give me the grace to follow you.

The Rainbow Of Patience

The rainbow of patience spans the whole gospel story. Jesus, patient and rich in mercy, waited for minds to listen, for hearts to open to his love.

When a town of Samaria refused to receive him, he would not call down fire and brimstone on it. His patience never ends. There would be another day when Philip would preach to the people of that town, and they opened their hearts. 'The multitudes with one accord gave heed to what was said by Philip.' (Acts 8:5)

There was the touching drama of flight and pursuit, which Jesus described in parable, and lived out in himself. The straying sheep, the sinner running, and the shepherd, impelled by love, ever pursuing, but never compelling. How vividly Francis Thompson captures that drama of patient pursuit:

But with unhurrying chase,
And unperturbed pace,
Deliberate speed, majestic instancy,
They beat – and a Voice beat
More instant than the Feet …

St Thomas Aquinas reminds us: 'If you are looking for patience you will find it in its highest form on the Cross. Through the darkness of his passion, his patience shines out. When he was struck on the face, he was silent. When false accusations were hurled against him, he held his peace.'

Our world is short in patience. There is a repeated petulant cry for instant solutions. Reliefs and answers must come, and they must come today.

To keep ourselves clear of the mood of impatience in the world around us, we can learn from the patience of Jesus, to bear the burdens and sorrows of life which test our patience.

> **The Lord, a God, merciful and gracious,**
> **patient and rich in mercy. (Ex 34:6)**

Heart of Jesus, patient and rich in mercy, have mercy on us.

The Reality Of Sin

It is the business of the Church to tell the world that there is forgiveness of sin. Right through the gospel Jesus cured all manner of diseases in reward for faith. 'Rise and go your way; your faith has healed you.' (Lk 17:19). So does he continue, through the Church, to heal us from the malady of sin.

Before availing of forgiveness we need to be aware of sin. Pope Pius XII described the sin of our world as the absence of the sense of sin. The world throws a cloak over sin. It goes its way as if sin did not exist, or uses soft, gentle words to describe it. Our faith enables us to keep alive a sense of shock, an awareness that sin is a reality, that it is still as horrible as the vision of the city of God in ruins, which caused Jesus to burst into tears.

Side by side with a sense of shock is a sense of wonder at the marvel of God's mercy. He speaks through remarkable messengers of mercy who have responded to the particular needs of our time. St Thérèse of the Child Jesus and St Faustina have made the divine mercy the centre of their lives, and the theme of their message to our world.

Blessed Padre Pio bore the wounds of Jesus on his body. He drew, and continues to draw countless souls to be cleansed in the sacrament of Penance. His daily prayer was centred on the Heart of Jesus, victim for sinners, our peace and our reconciliation. His whole life and apostolate were woven round the sacrament of Penance related to the holy Eucharist.

The more alive our recognition of the divine mercy, the more often we will be drawn to receive the sacrament of Penance.

Have mercy on me, God, in your kindness. (Ps 50:1)

Lord Jesus, grant me the grace to receive often and worthily the sacrament of Penance, so that I may grow in your love.

The Refugee Road

There is a painting by one of the great artists of the Flight into Egypt of Mary and Joseph with the child. He shows Mary seated on a path, with the child in her arms, and both are asleep while Joseph stands nearby. Just a moment's rest on their road to exile.

They have been described as 'the world's first refugees'. Strange paradox! The Son of God, coming as Emmanuel, God with us, and before his birth there was no room in the inn; and shortly afterwards, he is on the road to exile.

We have the story in detail: a sudden danger, an urgent call to rise up immediately in the night. 'Rise, take the child and his mother, and fly to Egypt.' (Mt 2:13) Out into the unknown and not knowing when they might return. 'Remain there till I tell you.' (Mt 2:13)

Did they not live the story of the world's refugees of our time? The same danger, urgency, uncertainty of that long, sad stream of exiles on the roads of our world. Through political upheavals, tribal wars, barred by colour or culture, with a few personal belongings on their backs, carrying their children in their arms, trying to help the aged along, driven forth on to what often seems the road to no place, leaving behind the smouldering ruins of their homes or villages.

Lest they appear as just an item on a news bulletin, we try to view them through the eyes and compassion of Jesus. 'I have compassion on the crowd ... I am unwilling to send them away hungry, lest they faint on the way.' (Mt 15:32) Thus our prayer goes out to the homeless multitudes, that either they find a home, or find an open road back to their homeland. And, as well, the support of our prayer to the army of heroic humanitarian helpers who are easing their burdens.

The Lord lifts up the downtrodden. (Ps 147:6)

Lord, give consolation and peace to the world's refugees.

The Reservoir

Sometimes a natural or artificially made lake supplies the vital need of water to a city. In the desert an oasis is the reservoir.

There is a divine source of life – the side of Jesus, opened on the Cross.

St Bonaventure gives us a line of thought in this context. We might describe the enrichment he gives us as under three headings: explanation, invitation, question.

He *explains:* 'That the Church might be formed from the side of Christ, "They shall look on him whom they have pierced", it was divinely appointed that one of the soldiers would pierce that sacred side, so that blood and water flowed out, the price of our salvation poured out from the fountain ...'

He *invites:* 'Arise, O soul, friend of Christ, watch without ceasing, bring hither thy mouth to drink of the waters from the Saviour's fountains.'

He *questions:* 'How could this burning love be better shown than that it permitted not only the body, but even the heart to be wounded by the spear?'

Who would not love that Heart so wounded?

Who can refuse to return the love of a heart so loving?

At once there came out blood and water. (Jn 19:34)

Heart of Jesus, fountain of life and holiness, have mercy on us.

The Road Back

There is a song with the title 'The Emigrant's Return', celebrating the joy of homecoming.

Like a strong rhythm, increasing in intensity, four words of the Prophet Isaiah, reach us – seek, call, forsake, return. Like a theme with variations, they express one thought – an urgent invitation to the sinner to take the road back.

All of us, by sin, have to some degree left our Father's house. But there need never be a point of no return. At some moment grace stirs us. Already a change of heart is bringing a change of direction. How do we proceed? The prophet tells us.

Seek: The honest search for God is never in vain. He shows us the way.

Call: We may feel that our prayer is but a plaintive cry. Yet ours is not a feeble call from the dark. We call with hope, for God is near.

Forsake: Well for us that God whom we have forsaken, whose Son was forsaken on the Cross, does not forsake us. All he asks is that we break with the past.

Return: The rest is easy. The road back is shorter. For our heavenly Father is already coming to greet us. We approach without fear, for we realise that he who loves us excessively '...will abundantly pardon' us.

> *Seek the Lord while he may be found ...*
> *For he will abundantly pardon. (Is 55:6, 7)*

> *Lord, help me to return to you with joy,*
> *to receive your pardon for my sins.*

The Scruple

There is a story in one of Canon Sheehan's novels of an old woman who came to the priest with a scruple. She explained: 'When I get tired of saying my beads I often make little plays to myself. I imagine I am at the door of the little house of Nazareth looking in, and I can hardly take my eyes off the Blessed Virgin and the child. And sometimes I ask her to let me do the jobs for her, to sweep the house. And sometimes I ask her to give me the child out of her arms, and she does. And now I want to know am I right or wrong. Am I making too free with God?'

'Dear Lord, what a scruple!' was the priest's reassuring reply.

Does not the gospel abound with incidents of making free with Jesus? Here and there along the road, without formality or introduction, a man or woman would rush forward into his presence.

A poor woman suffering from a long illness 'came up behind him and touched the fringe of his garment'. (Lk.8:44)

'And as he was setting out on his journey, a man ran up and knelt before him, and asked him, "Good Teacher, what must I do to inherit eternal life?" ' (Mk 10:17)

'... a Canaanite woman ... came out and cried, "Have mercy on me, O Lord, Son of David, my daughter is severely possessed by a demon."' (Mt 15:22)

As in the gospel, Jesus remains ever easy of access to us. We have no need to be afraid of making free with him.

I have taken them in my arms. (Hos 11:8)

Lord, bid me come to you.

The Simple Things Of Life

In an Intensive Care Unit of a hospital I saw a a patient, walking with the help of a stick. Each step he took very carefully and slowly. I said to him: 'It is good to be on your feet.' And his reply was: 'Father, one step at a time; the simple things of life.'

What a praiseworthy example of patience and appreciation, even of small mercies, was expressed in those few words! He deserved a prayer, and one felt that his cheerful acceptance would be sure to receive from the Lord his return to health.

He might not have been aware that another man, Cardinal Newman, struggling and suffering on his journey from darkness into the light of faith, had the same noble disposition:

'Keep thou my feet;I do not ask to see
The distant scene; one step enough for me.'

Isn't there a message here for all of us – 'the simple things of life' – the smaller pinpricks and hurts, those pains or stresses as well as those other simple things – a burst of sunshine after days of rain, a word or letter from a friend in time of need, those delicate gestures of love that touch our lives. For the painful moments, acceptance; for the joys, our thanks.

And then that gift of patience, so needed, but so elusive! We can make a start at gaining it – one step at a time.

I kept my feet firmly in your paths.
There was no faltering in my steps. (Ps 16:9)

Lord, I beg you to keep my steps on firm ground.
In your mercy, heal the sick.

The Stage of Memory

A phrase sometimes used is 'to bring the past on to the stage of memory' – by recall, to bring on stage a person, an event, an occasion of celebration, surrounded by happy memories, like the light of other days, brightening the present.

Such a kind of flashback can be occasioned by a photo of a dear one on the mantlepiece, a group photo on the wall, a video of a wedding celebration, that come alive across the span of years.

Sometimes that memory can be like a ray of light, brightening a dark hour.

St Peter experienced on Tabor a joy never to be forgotten, that one shining hour when the Lord shone like the sun. He never forgot that memory. Witness of a vision, 'eyewitnesses of his majesty', memory of his word, 'This is my beloved Son, with whom I am well pleased ... we were with him on the holy mountain.' (2 Pet 1:17, 18)

He was recalling this memory shortly before his death, and reminded his people to pay attention to this prophetic utterance, 'as to a lamp shining in a dark place'. (2 Pet 1:19)

The memory of Tabor is for us also, playing a light across every dark patch of our road.

I have remembered your name, Lord. (Ps 119:55)

Lord, help us to keep alive the memory of your love.

The Storm

A feature of the lake of Galilee is that sometimes, on a calm, warm evening, a violent cold wind sweeps down suddenly from Mount Hermon. Without warning it strikes the lake, and within minutes it stirs up a raging storm. Even fishermen with long experience of the lake cannot be forewarned.

Such a storm struck the little boat in which the apostles were crossing. The gospel describes the moment: 'And behold, there arose a great storm on the sea, so that the boat was being swamped by the waves.' (Mt 8:24) 'They roused Jesus who was asleep in the boat, crying out, "Save us, Lord, we are perishing." And he said to them: "Why are you afraid, O men of little faith?" He awoke and rebuked the wind and the sea; and there came a great calm.' (Mt 8:25, 27)

St Cyril comments: 'Together with the tempest of the waters he quelled the tempest of hearts.'

In our lives that kind of storm may sometimes hit us. Out of a blue sky, without warning, it comes in varied forms – maybe a medical diagnosis of a grave health condition, security of work falling apart, a deep upset, personal or family, a trying test of faith or hope.

In such a dark moment we too tend to cry out, like the apostles, for help, and again the gentle voice of Jesus will quell the storm.

You rule the raging of the sea. When its waves rise you still them.
(Ps 88:9)

Lord Jesus, give us faith and courage
when the tempests of life tend to engulf us.

The Supper

The painting of 'The Last Supper' by Leonardo da Vinci has been restored. The full beauty of this masterpiece is now clearly visible. One can admire the tenderness and majesty of the countenance of Jesus, the longing in the eyes of the apostles, all looking towards him.

By living the words that Jesus spoke on that night, the marvel of that occasion can come to life for us. His words, so simple, express so much.

'Having loved his own …' In choosing his apostles he made them his own. Some small vanities and shortcomings they had, but they were never short in love. He had made them to be with him, and every day in his company had brought a growth in their love.

Little did they realise how intimately he was going to become their possession through the new mystery of his love. They had left all things to give themselves to him. Now they were going to be re-warded, by receiving him, whole and entire, under the appearance of bread and wine.

'He loved them until the end....' The words present a panoramic vision of the Eucharist, through which Jesus loves until the end, not merely to the end of that night, nor to the end of life, but to the end of loving, to which there is no end. His heart, ever open in giving, found hearts ever open to receive.

We can apply the message to ourselves. When we open our hearts to him he makes us his own, and assures us that his love for us is never ending.

I have earnestly desired to eat this passover with you before I suffer.
(Lk 22:14)

Lord Jesus, help us, through the Eucharist,
to grow daily in your love.

The Testament

Before handing himself back to his Father, Jesus on the cross summoned up enough strength to hand over Mary and John to each other.

The great saints and artists have tried to express the pathos of that solemn moment, described in such simple words by St John: 'When Jesus saw his mother and the disciple whom he loved standing near, he said to his mother: "Woman, behold your son!" Then he said to the disciple: "Behold your mother!" And from that hour the disciple took her to his own home.' (Jn 19:26, 27)

It was the moment of the exchange. For her own son, Mary would receive John as her adopted son.

St Bernardine of Siena describes that moment: 'Which of us does not envy the beloved disciple who, to replace the absence of his Lord, was given the person of his mother? Can we not pray to him who died out of excessive love, to say to each of us: 'Behold your mother', and to her, 'Behold your son.'

In that moment Mary received her mission to be a spiritual mother of every member of the human family for all time. Wide as the arms of her son extended on the Cross are, her arms are strong and protective, gathering every one of us into her embrace. In the words of Manley Hopkins, 'She mantles the guilty globe.'

Blessed Pope John XXIII says that if we want to understand Mary, we must find her in the moment of the testament of the dying Jesus. He felt that we have not often enough repeated and reflected on the words: 'Behold your Mother.'

Do whatever he tells you. (Jn 2:5)

Mary, show yourself to me a mother.

The Three Roads

A thought of St John of the Cross: 'A man's footprints are the traces by which we can track him. The soul says to the Lord: I follow your footprints after the trace of your sweetness which you infuse and leave impressed on them.'

There are three roads related to the central mysteries of our salvation: the road of joy, to Ain Karim, the road of sorrow, to Jerusalem, and the road of glory, to Emmaus.

Jesus travelled to Ain Karim in the womb of his mother. It was high springtime with the first signs of life in nature greeting Mary. It was also the springtime of salvation. As David had sung with joy as he brought the Ark to Jerusalem, so did Mary raise her voice in a song of joy, glorifying the Lord her Saviour as she remembered his mercy.

Jesus travelled from Jericho to Jerusalem on his way to suffer and die and rise again. 'Behold we are going up to Jerusalem.' (Mk 9:33) He said his 'hour' was coming, the hour of his sacrifice. He was now going up the road that would lead to Calvary.

The third road is to Emmaus, The darkness of Calvary has ended, and the sunlight of Easter can never grow dim. The glory of the risen Lord is ever with us. Having recognised him in the breaking of bread we walk for ever a sunlit road in his presence. Thus, in the words of Cardinal Newman, 'We walk in sunlight even when in shadow.'

We would do well to travel those three roads often, keeping the memory of their history alive.

He ... followed him on the way. (Mk 10:52)

Lord Jesus grant me the grace ever to follow your footsteps.
Through the light of faith, may all people find their way to you.

The Trellis

The long branches of the vine can stretch out several feet from the parent vine, and are supported as they cling on to a trellis. The sap reaches from the vine to the utmost tips of the branches.

St Ambrose gives us a vivid image: 'Just as the vine embraces the trellis so the Lord Jesus, like the eternal vine, embraces his people with arms of love, as it were.' There is the idea of the vine clinging closely to the trellis, an image of the Lord, so loving us that he clings to us to hold us in his embrace. We, in turn, cling to him. 'My soul clings to you.' (Ps 62:8)

There is a sense of intimacy we experience in his eucharistic presence. We do not come as strangers from the world outside. He greets us as he welcomes his apostles at the last supper: 'I have called you friends.' (Jn 15:15)

The more we articulate our faith in the marvel of his presence, the more we want to cling to him, to hold him close.

On Easter day the women came up and took hold of his feet and worshipped him (Mt 28:9) and were rewarded. 'Do not be afraid.' (Mt 28:10)

In your presence I learn to touch you and beg you to touch me with your healing power. The women at Easter travelled to you, 'They came up'. I also travel to your presence, asking for the faith of those women, so that I may be worthy to hold you, like the vine to the trellis, and worship you.

I am the vine, you are the branches. (Jn 15:15)

Lord, grant me the grace to come ever closer to you
so as to live through love in your presence.

The Wedding

There is a delightful one act play in Irish, *An Pósadh*, which is built round the story of a young newly married couple. Both of them are poor, and their home is little more than a tiny cabin almost without furnishings.

A poor man who is a travelling fiddler comes along, and as he stands at the open door of their home he plays, tune after tune. And while he plays, people pass along the road. Some stop to listen, and many of the passers-by put a coin in his cap at his feet.

When he has finished playing, he takes the coins from his cap and gives them to the couple, and goes on his way. They offer him their deep thanks, which is all they have to give.

Here is a touching story of love that goes out. One is reminded of the words of Giovanni Papini: 'Love is a fire that goes out unless we communicate it to others.'

In a world that is often more intent on having than on giving, this little play has a message. It is a message so often repeated by Pope John Paul II – the need of a social love that goes out to those who have needs, whether spiritual or material.

Beloved, let us love one another. (1 Jn 4:7)

Lord, help us to be generous to those in need.

The Winepress Alone

To travel a long, dark road by night could lower one's spirits. To journey alone, would be an added burden.

Was ever a road so lonely as the journey of Jesus from Gethsemane to Calvary?

He had come into the world to bring companionship, and as he was about to face the ordeal in the garden he asked for the presence of friends. But it was the hour of darkness, and he was seized, and from then there was no friend in sight. 'All the disciples forsook him and fled.' (Mt 26:56)

Through all that night and morning, there was never a voice to comfort him, never a word in his defence. Only calumnies and falsehoods and an orgy of venemous words, and cries shouting for his death.

But, however wounded and weakened, he would go forward, because he willed it. He went out, 'bearing his own cross', (Jn 19:17) the only property left to him.

There was just one brief moment of comfort, from women who 'bewailed and lamented him.' (Lk 23:27) And beneath the cross, there was the final and treasured companionship of his mother with John and Magdalene.

Truly it is called the *Via Dolorosa*. But the hour of darkness ended, and the splendid sunshine of Easter played on that road.

And for all time, whether in Jerusalem or in Christian churches, lovers of Jesus crucified travel that road. Not only with their feet, but with their hearts they follow him, and with tears and love they mourn him and they offer their crosses to him in reparation for the sins of the world.

I have trodden the winepress alone. (Is 63:3)

Lord Jesus, I beg you to give the comfort of your presence to all who feel alone through a night of pain, or through the loneliness of depression.

They Shall Look

The final line of the drama of Calvary conveys an invitation to look. 'They shall look on him whom they have pierced.' (Jn 19:37) Love has eyes. We look with love on Jesus crucified and, because we have pierced him, our love will be all the deeper.

St Paul's love was so intense that he wanted to be crucified with Christ. Just one phrase of his will be enough to enliven our love of Jesus in the supreme proof of his love. 'He loved me and gave himself for me.' (Gal 2:20) I stand alone before the Cross. For me he offered his life. To me he gave his love without limit. All the saints are lovers of the Cross, in varied forms of expression.

St Catherine of Siena longed to stay close to the sacred wounds of Jesus so that she might drink his Precious Blood lest it might fall to the ground.

St Paul of the Cross used to cry out, 'O my most loving God, what you suffered for me! What insults, what injuries, you who were not just any person, but the Son of God!'

St John of the Cross reflected on the thirst of Jesus and on the unfathomable spring of love from his side. 'This thirst so exhausts the soul that she would think nothing of breaking through the midst of the camp of the Philistines, as did David's strong men to fill their containers with water from the cistern of Bethlehem which was Christ.' (1 Par 11, 18)

St Teresa Benedicta Stein's favourite prayer was, 'Hail, O Cross, our only hope.'

What can I do? Pascal reminds me that 'Christ is in his agony till the end of the world, so we must not be idle.' When some one in his Body, the Church, has a cross to bear, perhaps I could lend a hand to ease the burden.

Bear one another's burdens. (Gal 6:2)

Lord Jesus, help me to love you
in return for all that you have suffered for love of me.

Thirsting For Love

A person in a raging fever can suffer an intense pain of thirst. A soldier wounded in battle, suffering from loss of blood, cries out in agony for even one drop of water on his lips.

On the Cross Jesus cried out in agony, 'I thirst.' (Jn 19:28) In his fifth word from the Cross, for the first time through all his intense pain during his sacred passion, he spoke of his suffering.

St Gregory Nazianzen explains that 'I thirst' means ' I thirst to be thirsted for'. His deepest thirst was to be loved. No greater love could he give than his life, and so in that cry from his heart he longed for a response. His deepest desire then, and till the end of time, would remain to be loved.

He had already foretold that he would draw hearts. 'And I, when I am lifted up from the earth, will draw all men to myself.' (Jn 12:32) The one motive that would draw, would be to be drawn by love. The first verse of the Canticle describes how the beloved is so overcome by the love she has received, she wishes for nothing more than to be drawn. 'Draw me after you.' (Cant 1:1)

Jesus plants the desire to love him in human hearts, which creates the desire to love him in return.

The great mosaics often depict the harts slaking their thirst at the fountain. 'As a hart longs for running streams, so my soul is longing for you, my God.' (Ps 42:1)

St John Chrysostom throws light on the motive that most draws us to make a return of love:

'There is nothing which so draws a man to return love, as when he understands that he who loves him is urgently longing for his affection. The greatest power of love is that, when spurned, the one who loves is willing to live and die with the beloved.'

If any one thirst, let him come to me and drink. (Jn 7:37)

Lord Jesus, create in my heart a thirst to love you,
and to open my heart to those who come to me for food and drink.

Tides

Each day the precise times of tides are recorded in weather charts,

We marvel at how the sea, when it reaches full tide, comes to a line, almost as yesterday, and then recedes.

We need not be surprised, because the Lord has told us that he has set limits to the waters that they would not flow onwards and engulf us. 'You have set limits which they should not pass.' (Ps 103:9)

But there are other limits that tend to frighten us. There are times when we seem to have reached the limit of endurance. Fear itself seems to step across our reserves of courage. Times when pain tests us to the limit. Times when the menacing tide of temptation seems to engulf us.

At such moments, Lord, you reassure us, reminding us how you stop the tides and the waters obey you, how, with one gesture, you bade the storm to abate on the lake of Galilee.

Why, then, should we doubt that you will ever allow any tide to crowd in on us and engulf us?

The Lord ... 'who shut in the sea with doors'. (Job 38:8)

Lord Jesus, keep us safe from those tidal waves in life
that tend to envelop us.

Tired From The Journey

As we travel our daily road, often we feel weary. The burden of living, the wear and tear of life, the painful hurts pull us down.

What a consolation to turn to that gospel story where Jesus was tired from the journey. Along parched dusty roads, through valleys and over hills, beneath a scorching sun, he had travelled till, overcome by fatigue, he sat down by a well

A woman, coming to the well for water, found him, not seated on a throne but on the ground. His simple request to her: 'Give me a drink,' (Jn 4:7) started a dialogue. Ever so gently he took her back along her sinful history till her heart was melted. He told her of a deeper well of water springing up to eternal life.

Now it was the woman who thirsted. 'Sir, give me this water that I may not thirst.' (Jn 4:15)

It was about the sixth hour (Lk 23:44), the same hour when Jesus, tired from another journey, lay down on the Cross.

St Augustine brings the threads of the story together: 'He asked her for a drink, and promised to give her a drink. He is in need as one who will accept; he abounds as one who will satisfy.'

Whoever drinks of the water I shall give him will never thirst.
(Jn 4:14)

Lord, give me your help when I am weary.
Ease the burden of all those who, on the road of life,
are tired from the journey.

To Give And To Belong

The Song of Songs describes in poetic language the bond between the lover and the beloved: 'I to my beloved and my beloved to me.' (Song 2:16)

Here is a summary of all my striving, the whole purpose of my life. I give myself to my beloved – totally and exclusively. No one outside him, no interest outside him.

Such daring on my part – to dare to possess my beloved. Only by a total humility, an absolute admission of my nothingness, can I ever make bold to call him 'Beloved', to dream of having him as my own.

St Gregory of Nyssa says the phrase from the Canticle means 'that I possess nothing but God alone, and must look for nothing outside him'. The Bride, in saying 'I to my beloved', declares that she has modelled herself on Christ, thus recovering her own proper loveliness. Every finding of you is a refinding, opening a vision and a motive for a new song.

Lord, I try to see the beauty of this union as an advance revelation of the sublime union which you have promised me, if only I open my heart totally to you.

Abide in me and I in you. (Jn 15:4)

Lord, open my heart to your love.

To Stay With Jesus

Often on the occasion of a visit between friends, one would say to the other: 'Would you not stay a little longer'? The words 'stay', 're-main', 'abide', convey the idea of congenial, reposeful presence.

The theme 'stay' is like a golden thread that is woven into the gospel of St John. We find it in three settings.

Responding to the invitation of Jesus, 'Come and see,' 'they stayed with him that day'. (Jn 1:39) That was an evening to remember for the rest of their lives. In the intimacy and joy of that evening in his presence they became his own. Their hearts were set aglow with love for him.

A night more memorable still came when Jesus gathered his own for the last supper. 'One of the disciples whom Jesus loved was lying close to the breast of Jesus.' (Jn 13:23) What an experience, to stay so close that he could feel the heart beat of Jesus!

It was for him to record the language of desire in the love discourse of Jesus. 'As the Father has loved me, so have I loved you. Abide in my love.' (Jn 15:9) St Augustine explains that the words mean 'abide in the love I have for you'. Nothing could be more permanent than the love which Jesus bestows.

That is the marvel of his eucharistic presence. He 'stays' for our sake. He allows us to come close to him as did St John, to become ever more vividly aware of his love for us. There we can pour out to him the thoughts and needs of our hearts. When we live close to his heart, he rewards us. What a reward! St John Eudes tells us how we are enriched: 'All that he has is yours, his spirit, his heart, his body, his soul, all his faculties, all are to be used by you as if they were your own, so that, serving him, you may praise him, love him, glorify him.'

He who abides in me, and I in him, he it is that bears much fruit.
(Jn 15:5)

Lord Jesus, grant me the joy of staying close to you. May I grow ever more aware of and grateful to you for your eucharistic presence.

Today

What a wonderful word is 'today'. Silent as the dawn it comes, and almost without notice its hours tick over, and then, just as noiselessly it slips beneath the setting sun, and is gone.

This is how we find it in the gospel – majestic events enclosed between sunrise and sunset. The news broke upon the world that the night had gone, and a new world began.

A new day had come with the announcement that today is born a Saviour.

And as the sun darkened on Calvary, the word 'today' resounded in the heart of a poor criminal. All he had pleaded for was to be remembered, and what a reward: 'today with me in Paradise'!

Every day between dawn and dusk we travel a stretch of the road. This precious gift of today, how do we use it? Often we tend to live in a kind of nostalgia for yesterday. If only I could have it back, I would sort things out differently. We burden ourselves with memories of our wasted yesterdays.

We can be tempted to live in a world of dreams of a possible Utopia tomorrow. The world advertises tomorrow – the eternal 'mañana' when a fortune may come our way.

Pope John Paul II has useful advice. 'Time is not a journey into nothingness, but a journey to eternity. The real danger is not to the passing of time, but using it badly.'

Today, if you would listen to his voice, harden not your hearts.
(Heb 3:7)

Lord, grant me the grace to love you every moment of today.

Two Bridges

There are two bridges which are related to important moments of history. One, the bridge across the Tiber called the Ponte Sant Angelo, leading on to St Peter's; the other, O'Connell Bridge, Dublin.

The Roman bridge, also called the Bridge of Salvation, Bernini thought of as making access from the secular city to a holy place. Great statues of angels, each holding an instrument of the passion, on either side of the bridge, while nearby a great bronze statue of St Michael the Archangel, to guard the city and the Church.

Across that bridge on the occasion of the first Holy Year, in 1300, pilgrims walked in solemn procession.

O'Connell Bridge is the central link that joins two parts of a city into one. It also can evoke a memory which is a link of faith. An important moment of its history was that solemn moment when an altar was placed there around which a million people gathered in an act of eucharistic worship at the close of the International Eucharistic Congress in 1932.

It recalled, also, an important memory to a people who only three years before had celebrated the centenary of the attainment of Catholic emancipation.

Both bridges recall a conviction of what is central to our faith – that the Eucharist is the source and summit of our Christian faith. Jesus is the Bridge Builder who, through his Passion and Death and Resurrection, sacramentally renewed in the Eucharist, has made a passage bringing us across from death to life.

They gathered the church together
and declared all that God had done with them. (Acts 14:14).

Lord, strengthen our awareness of your presence in the holy Eucharist.

Two Messengers Of Mercy

From the same region of Poland, and near in time, have come two great messengers of mercy – St Faustina and Pope John Paul II. Just a few thoughts of theirs may help us to explore the mystery of mercy.

Vivid words of theirs express the need, in our world, of a revelation of the Lord, who is rich in mercy, and, as well, the drawing power of mercy which brings human hearts near to the heart of the Saviour. Both of them, their hearts centred on the love of Jesus, were able to present to us, in words simple yet sublime, the riches of his divine mercy.

St Faustina: 'Jesus, I want to bring souls to the fount of your mercy to draw the reviving water of life with the vessal of trust.'

'I join all my sufferings to yours, and deposit them in the treasury of the Church for the benefit of souls.'

'O wound of mercy, heart of Jesus, hide me in your own blood, and do not let me out for ever.'

Pope John Paul II: 'Mercy is, as it were, love's second name.'

'The generous face of mercy has to be ever revealed anew.'

'The Cross is like the touch of eternal love on the most painful wounds of man's earthly existence.'

How many painful wounds have nations, families, individuals suffered in our time, who have urgent need of the touch of eternal love, and have been consoled and healed by the gift of the divine mercy!

To plead for mercy is our daily need; to thank the Lord for his mercy is the highest expression of our love.

The Lord is merciful and gracious,
slow to anger and abounding in steadfast love. (Ps 102:8)

Lord, I trust in your divine mercy.
In the abundance of your mercy, forgive us our sins.

Undimmed Memory

What a gift is memory! It gives us the power of recognition, it cements friendships, it keeps hearts open to live in a mood of thanksgiving. For even by a small keepsake we can keep alive the memory of a friend. We remember past favours and are grateful.

Memory enriches. But what a painful impoverishment is loss of memory! Such an isolation it causes! A person who is loved becomes almost a stranger.

Loss of memory is a privation of health. But, in the wider sense, our world, in many ways, suffers from dimmed memory. When life centres on self, then the other person can be less remembered.

It is so easy to forget something which we deeply need to remember – that we, like the people of God of old, tend to forget. We need to be reminded, that it is the same God who constantly remembers us with love, feeding us, protecting us, keeping us safe from the hazards of the road.

What a powerful assurance of God's tender memory are the words of the prophet: 'Can a woman forget her sucking child, that she should have no compassion on the son of her womb? Even these may forget, yet I will not forget you.' (Is 49:14, 15)

Jesus gave us the Eucharist, directing us to remember: 'Do this in remembrance of me.' (Lk 22:19) Could we ever forget?

The Lord remembers his mercy for ever. (Ps 93:7)

Lord, I thank you for remembering me and all who feel forgotten.

Up From The Dust

In one of those tragic moments of World War Two, the Benedictine monastery of Monte Cassino was destroyed. A wave of bombers descended on it and in a few moments it lay, a massive pile of broken masonry.

It was a sight that brought to mind the words 'How the pure gold is changed! The holy stones lie scattered ...' (Lam 4:1)

But patient and artistic hands got to work and when their task was done, the monastery arose in all its original splendour, as if it had never been destroyed.

As I approached the main entrance to the church after it had been rebuilt, through the open door came the sound of the singing of vespers by the community. And the verse I heard was: 'I will praise the Lord at all times.' (Ps 33:1)

The words summarised the framework of the monastic way of life which St Benedict founded. Keep the praise of God, 'the work of God', at the centre. They also may be thought of as a central theme of a melody that has echoed through so many moments of history, presenting a new vision, through the Benedictine way of life, when the Christian life and even civilisation itself seemed to be falling apart.

The whole story has a message for each of us. 'At all times', like that monastic community, if I bless the Lord, even in moments of distress, I can be sure that he will lift me up from the dust.'

I will rebuild its ruins, and I will set it up. (Acts 15:16)

Lord, help me to rebuild my faith and courage
when I am broken by the battles of life.

Wanting For Nothing

A highly qualified nurse, who had served her profession with distinction as well as devoting care to pilgrimage invalids, herself became an invalid.

When I asked her during her illness how she was, she replied, 'I receive Holy Communion every day. What more could I want?'

Her impressive words bring to mind a key phrase in the shepherd psalm: 'The Lord is my shepherd, I shall not want.' (Ps 23:1)

The sense of security of 'not wanting' derives from the awareness of the shepherd's care. It is because of his tender care and thought for all my needs that I want for nothing.

The shepherd has a personal care of the sheep. He knows them by name, he preserves them from danger, he finds pasture for them.

They want for nothing. Like the people on the hillside: 'And they all ate and were satisfied.' (Mt 14:20) They wanted for nothing.

There is also assurance for the future. 'I shall not want.' The care given today will also be there tomorrow.

We can read this psalm in the context of the Eucharist. Here is the Shepherd ever present, ever tending his flock. Every time we come into his presence he would have us 'lie down', to be at rest and at ease from the turmoil of life. He would provide new 'pastures', new experiences of his consolation, encouragement, a table laden with good things, and a certainty of home 'for ever'.

I am the good shepherd. (Jn 10:11)

Lord Jesus, draw me often into your presence,
where I may adore, praise and thank you without ceasing.

Watch For Boredom

An American named Kaplan took up the study of one symphony by Mahler. It was the only piece of music he learned, and he perfected the art of conducting it. He became a conductor of world class conducting that symphony, and has been invited to conduct the great orchestras of the world.

Once he was asked how he avoided becoming bored with conducting just this one work. He answered: 'No. What Mahler is presenting is life, death and purpose; and you don't get bored with those concepts.'

Interesting that when God, out of sheer love, fed his people every day of forty years with manna, they became bored. 'There is nothing at all for us but this manna to look at.' (Num 11:6)

How can we keep clear of boredom? The answer is wonderment. Something more marvellous than the manna in the desert has been given to us, the Bread of Life, to sustain us every day of our desert journey. 'O wonderful thing, the poor and humble servant is nourished by the Lord, with food!'

O res mirabilis! Manducat Dominum pauper servus et humilis.

*Lord, help me to admire, appreciate, and adore
your wondrous gift of the Eucharist*

Welcome Home

When setting up a home on the occasion of marriage, a couple begin by putting together the basic furnishings that give it comfort and a sense of welcome – some carpeting, curtains, a picture on the wall, a vase of flowers. It might be just a one-roomed apartment, but it is home.

For the liturgy of the Nuptial Mass they often choose readings from St Paul. Writing to the Colossians, he lists the qualities that might be called the basic furnishings of a Christian home – compassion, kindness, patience, forgiveness, readiness to forgive a hurt, and 'above all, put on love.' (Col 3:12, 13)

Those virtues give a home the warmth of welcome and comfort that bind the members 'together in perfect harmony'. (Col 3:14)

That ideal becomes reality when there is some prayer, no matter how short, in the home. The family that prays sustains the holiness and permanence of marriage.

It's good to come home, to be home. Monsignor Ronald Knox describes that feeling. Coming into a truly Christian home 'is like coming in to warm your hands at the fire on a cold day.'

Where two or three are gathered together in my name, there am I in the midst of them. (Mt 18:20)

Lord, bless all families with love and peace.
Give the members the grace to pray together.

When Love Was Betrayed

Caravaggio used his unique gifts in his painting of 'The taking of Christ', the moment in Gethsmane when Jesus was taken prisoner.

It was the night when he was betrayed, the night of love's summit, which was also the hour of darkness.

It is useful for us to look well on this painting. It can draw us closer to that scene which has evoked the love of countless human hearts. The artist used a device, 'chiaroscuro', the strong contrast between light and shadow, which is here the symbol of the contrast between love and betrayal.

We notice the gesture of hands. The hand of Judas, hard and crusted, grasps the right arm of Jesus. The hand of a solder reaches forward to clasp his shoulder. And, in the background, a hand is raised up high, pointing towards Jesus, as if to indicate 'this is he'. But, most striking, the hands of Jesus are clasped as in as gesture of prayer. His hands are free, as his heart is free to accept the chalice of suffering. St Ambrose comments: 'Jesus was bound, not by knotted ropes, but he is drawn close by chains of love.'

On the countenance of Jesus there is no fear, but a most serene peace. Violent hands are laid on him, but he does not resist. He goes because he wills it.

They came up and laid hands on Jesus and seized him. (Mt 26:50)

Lord Jesus, free us from sin,
so that we may be united to you with the bonds of love.

Where The Beams Meet

St Paul was a master of language, and he used all his skill to express in words the love of Christ. Like an expert painter he was able to depict Christ crucified in words centering on his heart: '... the breadth and length and height and depth.' (Eph 3:18) The Fathers of the Church interpreted those words as a picture in words depicting the beams:

the horizontal beam – the breadth and length;

the vertical beam –the height and depth;

and, where the beams meet – there is the heart.

Do we not find a similar word picture in the opening part of the third Eucharistic Prayer in the Mass? What a fitting introduction to our final preparation for the central part of the Mass where we find the love of Christ 'which surpasses knowledge'! (Eph 3:19)

The vertical movement: 'Father, all life, all holiness comes from you through your Son, Jesus Christ.' The horizontal: 'you gather a people to yourself, so that from east to west a perfect offering may be made to the glory of your name.'

The downward movement of life from the Father to us through Jesus Christ, and then the majestic sweep of inclusion, from east to west, the outstretched arms of Jesus on the Cross.

Again, where the beams meet is where an assembled people find the heart of the Saviour.

To me this grace was given
to preach the unsearchable riches of Christ. (Eph 3:5)

Lord, help me to find in your heart the riches of your love.
Draw all hearts to yourself.

Who Else Would Love?

The poet, Francis Thompson, put on your lips, Lord, a question. 'Whom wilt thou find to love ignoble thee, save me, save only me?

In spite of your infinite love, and my feeble response; in spite of your infinite patience with my impatience, you keep on loving me.

Who but you would look beneath the dust and defilements that darken my soul, and find there and rejoice in the faded image of your beauty that remains?

I may have lost the world's esteem. I may have become even a castaway in the dust heap. Maybe I have to feel abandoned in order to realise that you do not love and then abandon.

The fallen leaves of autumn make the spring fruitful. The time has come for me to surrender to you, Lord. Burn away what is of me in me. Through a little suffering that you offer me, purify and warm this heart of mine in the crucible of your suffering.

St John of the Cross tells me how to put my prayer into words:
O flame of living love
That dost eternally
Pierce through my soul
With so consuming heat,
Make thou an end of me.
O burn that burns to heal!
O more than pleasant wound!

I have loved you with an everlasting love. (Jer 31:3)

Lord, make me love you more and more.

Widen Your Hearts

One of the tragic contradictions of the coming of Jesus into the world to enfold all hearts in the embrace of his love was that there was no room for him in the inn. A world closed in on itself was more concerned with having than with giving.

The mood of our world is no different. The advice of St Paul to the Corinthians we might take as directed to ourselves to help us: 'Our heart is wide. You are not restricted by us but by your affections. In return, I speak to children; widen your hearts also.' (2 Cor 6:11, 12).

We might bring that advice to bear on our prayer in the eucharistic presence of Jesus. Certainly, we pray in praising and pleading for our selves. But ensure that we broaden the horizons of our prayer. We make room in our hearts for all those in the world outside to whom his heart goes out, in that flotsam and jetsam of life, where there is brokenness of heart, poverty, homelessness, a spiritual exhaustion from a lessening of faith, hope or love. Widen our hearts; make room for them in the inn of our hearts; make space for them in our prayer.

We make our own the prayer of St Faustina: 'O Jesus, I understand that your mercy is beyond all imagining and, therefore, I ask you to make my heart so big that there will be room in it for the needs of all the souls living on the face of the earth.'

**You shall not harden your heart
or shut your hand against your poor brother. (Deut 15:7)**

Lord Jesus, open my heart with compassion for all in need.

Wings That Lift

An aircraft depends on wings to become airborne. They are necessary for ascent and for maintaining altitude.

All our efforts in prayer have to start with a take off, an upward movement of ascent, a turning of our minds and efforts upwards towards God.

That is how the *Catechism of the Catholic Church* introduces its chapter on prayer. It uses a quotation from St Thérèse of Lisieux:

'For me, prayer is a surge of the heart; it is a simple look turned toward heaven; it is a cry of recognition and of love, embracing both trial and joy.'

The starting point is not from the heights of our pride but from the depths, from humility.

Dante in the last Canto of his *Paradiso,* describes our need of Mary's help in order to start the ascent in prayer. Without her help we would be trying the impossible – to fly without wings.

'Lady, you are so great and have such worth,

that any one who would wish to have grace

without having recourse to you,

would be desiring to fly without wings.'

Mary is the Virgin who prays (the *Virgo orans*). With confidence we ask her to help us to make the surge of the heart, and upward glance.

To you, O Lord, I lift up my soul; I trust you;
let me not be disappointed. (Ps 24:1)

Mary, help me to pray, and to be constant in glorifying the Lord.

With A Whole Heart

To love just for the sake of loving, that is love at its highest. St Augustine gives us an example: 'A raven feeds her young. She does not say, "I feed them so that they will feed me in my old age." She feeds because she loves.'

God, a loving Father, fed his people, protected them and opened to them a land of promise, just because he loved. Despite their failures, infidelities, ingratitude, there was never a moment when his love was withdrawn. And all that he asked from them was love, a wholehearted love. 'You shall love the Lord your God with all your heart.' (Deut 6:15)

Jesus completed the revelation of total giving. He shed the last drop of his blood, to draw all things to himself, just in order to be loved. He had no more to give. Who, therefore had more right to ask, 'My son, give me your heart.' (Ps 23:26)

But total giving does not come easy to us. We give a little here and there. As Cardinal Newman puts it: 'We promise all, but give by halves.' So often we have a secret compartment in our hearts into which no one, not even Jesus, may enter. There can be a little selfishness, a little indulgence which we must have, and we keep them under lock and key, our bit of private property. In the words of Francis Thompson: 'Lest, having him, I must have naught beside.'

We readily plead with all our hearts: 'With my whole heart I seek you.' Would that we could as truthfully say: 'With my whole heart I love you.'

You shall love the Lord your God with all your heart,
and with all your soul, and all your strength. (Mk 12:30)

Lord Jesus, give me a generous heart,
so that my one object in life may be to love you
and to make you loved.